CCSN LIBRARY

D0601185

FEB 01 2010

The Educated Franchisee

The How-To Book for

Choosing a Winning Franchise

The Educated Franchisee

The How-To Book for

Choosing a Winning Franchise

by Rick Bisio
written with Mike Kohler

www.educatedfranchisee.com

Copyright © 2008 by Rick Bisio. All rights reserved.

Bascom Hill Publishing Group
212 3rd Avenue North, Suite 570
Minneapolis, MN 55401
612-455-2293
www.bascomhillpublishing.com

All rights reserved. No part of this publication may be reproduced, stored in a retrieval system, or transmitted, in any form or by any means, electronic, mechanical, photocopying, recording, or otherwise, without the written prior permission of the author.

ISBN 13: 978-0-9798467-7-9
ISBN 10: 0-9798467-7-3
LCCN - 2007942122

Book sales for North America and international:
Itasca Books, 3501 Highway 100 South, Suite220
Minneapolis, MN 55416
Phone: 952.345.4488 (toll free 1.800.901.3480)
Fax: 952.920.0541; email to orders@itascabooks.com

Cover Design by Meghan Gale and George Louli
Typeset by Peggy LeTrent

Printed in the United States of America

PRAISE FOR *THE EDUCATED FRANCHISEE*

"Rick has rewritten the expression 'live and learn' to say 'study, learn ... and earn.'
For someone thinking about business ownership, that approach is more powerful
and relevant." – **DAVID G. MCKINNON** – IFA Entrepreneur of the Year – 2001, Co-
Founder, CEO and Chairman of Service Brands International (Molly Maid, Mr. Handyman,
1-800-Dry Clean, Ductz Air Duct Cleaning)

"Becoming a business owner is scary, and for good reason if you don't know exactly
what to do to be successful. The Educated Franchisee takes stress out of the process
and gives you everything you need to make confident, smart decisions. This book
will be your most valuable ally as you discover the lucrative and exciting world of
franchise ownership." – **LARINA KASE** – PsyD MBA New York Times bestselling
coauthor of *The Confident Speaker* and Business Coach to franchisees

"Fear is a good motivator. So is wealth. This book shows they can work together to
help you find success as an entrepreneur in franchising." – **FRANK CARNEY** – Co-
Founder Pizza Hut - Current Franchisee Papa John's Pizza

"The power of knowledge when met with the ability to dream come together in a
fantastic roadmap that is The Educated Franchisee. Whether it is understanding
what makes a good entrepreneur or, taking that a step further, what makes a good
franchise, this book gives a frank and honest picture of dreams in a very real world
of possibilities; the world of business and franchising. Read and learn." – **DINA**
DWYER-OWENS – Chairwoman and CEO, The Dwyer Group

"If you're wondering whether it's time for a change in life – this is a must read! It's
filled with insights and useful nuggets of information. Let Rick's experience and
wisdom be your guide to understanding how to harness the power of franchising."
– **LORI KISER-BLOCK** – President, FranChoice, Inc.

"Rick Bisio's effort to help prospective franchise investors gain the education and
knowledge they need to enter the exciting world of franchising is an important
undertaking in a rapidly-growing industry. His experience as a franchise
professional gives him special insights into the needs of those new to franchising."
– **MATTHEW R. SHAY** – President, International Franchise Association

"As a new franchisee, the knowledge and teaching Rick shares in this book is invaluable. In many ways becoming an entrepreneur is like going into space - the better you prepare, the lower the risk. This book will help you plan for a safe and exciting voyage." — **ANDY ALLEN** — NASA Astronaut (Pilot 1992 and 1994, Mission Commander 1996), Top Gun Pilot, Franchisee of BounceU

"The Educated Franchisee is a 'must read' for anyone thinking about or actively pursuing a franchise business. Read it and save yourself enormous amounts of time and money!" — **JOHN HEWITT** is the Founder and CEO of Liberty Tax Service, Co-Founder of Jackson Hewitt Tax Service and the IFA Entrepreneur of the Year 2006. Mr. Hewitt is the only individual to have founded two top 10 ranked franchise systems.

"The Educated Franchisee provides the small businessperson the tools to achieve 'The American Dream' of successful ownership. Rick's approach makes it easy to take the journey toward wealth creation. A must read for any potential franchisee!" — **JON LUTHER** — Chairman and Chief Executive Officer of Dunkin Brands, Former President of Popeyes Chicken and Biscuits, Winner of the IMFA 2007 Gold Plate Award, Chain Leader's 2006 Leadership award and Nation's Restaurant News Golden Chain Award

"From the psychology of success to financing alternatives – it is all here. Powerfully written in a no nonsense style. If The Educated Franchisee cannot get you there, no book will! Rick Bisio has coached thousands of people to wonderful life decisions - including me." — **FORD KYES** — ActionCOACH Firm franchisee owner and former CEO, St. Anthony's Health Care, St. Petersburg, Florida

Acknowledgements

Often what you know is significantly less important than having the right people around you, supporting you and providing you with great advice. In that regard, I have been blessed. This book simply would not have happened without the support of several key people.

The first person to thank is my wife, Anne-Lise. It was through your vision that the idea of a book was created and through your willingness to sacrifice that I was able to find the time to make this book happen. I also thank you for your editing, layout, proofing and research. You are my one and only.

In addition, I thank Mike Kohler for sticking with me during this process and putting up with my constant need to "improve" the book. Your patience, wisdom and hard work over the past 18 months have allowed this book to mature and evolve. I have great respect for you. You can be proud of your work.

There have been a number of other people that have been exceptionally supportive. I thank Britt Schroeter, Stephen Hogan and Patty Norman for their willingness to spend countless hours critiquing early versions of this book. Your work has significantly improved the book. I also thank Diane Pleuss for her guidance and effort in final editing and proofreading.

I also wish to thank all the folks at FranChoice, both in the corporate office and the consultant base. You are some for the most experienced, thoughtful, and supportive people I have ever come to know. I thank each of you for your willingness to share your ideas and approaches over the years. Whether you know it or not, you are reflected in this book.

Finally, I would like to thank my parents. You have shown me how to work hard while maintaining a high sense of integrity. You have significantly contributed to my love of business ownership and to my appreciation of family. It is through your example that I build success as an entrepreneur and as a person.

Foreword

If Rick Bisio wanted to be a "salesman," I have no doubt that he would be a great one. In fact, I'm sure he would be a rousing success at whatever he set his mind to, but I think of the sales arena specifically because of the balance Rick brings to his craft.

Balance is what makes Rick an outstanding teacher.

Rick understands – and I'm sure it's instinctive – where lines are to be drawn. He exudes optimism, without being "salesy." He's action-oriented, without being pushy. Best of all, Rick's a great sounding board because of a winning formula: active listening followed by thought-provoking feedback. In other words, he doesn't just tell people what they want to hear; he makes them consider what they need to hear.

If you look strictly at Rick's track record, the numbers instantly proclaim the obvious. He's been one of the country's most successful franchise consultants for years. However, that snapshot alone doesn't explain how balance is instrumental in Rick's work.

Balance stems from Rick's well rounded experiences, traits that portray deeper dimensions of Rick and his work. The numbers *tell* Rick is successful. Probing below the surface tells *why* he is so successful.

His history includes roles ranging from teacher to franchisee to corporation executive to entrepreneur. And all of those roles are marked by high achievement.

That's why I was delighted to learn that Rick had chosen to share his knowledge through the publishing of a book. I know it's what he loves to do: *share knowledge*. While other consultants have clients, Rick has students. By sharing openly with his students, he helps them make great business decisions about business ownership.

And wouldn't you know it; among all those great business decisions, you just happen to find an amazing roster of tremendously successful franchisees!

—Don DeBolt

Don DeBolt *is former president of the International Franchise Association (IFA) (1995 to 2004), one of the world's oldest and largest trade associations representing the franchise community, and is a co-author of <u>Street Smart Franchising</u>. He has served as a member of the Committee of 100 and the Public Affairs Committee of the U.S. Chamber of Commerce; a member of the Department of Commerce's Industry Sector Advisory Committee on Wholesaling and Retailing for Trade Policy Matters; sat on the board of directors of the Small Business Legislative Council and the National Cooperative Bank's Retail Finance Corporation; and was a member of the National Congress for Community Economic Development Advisory Council.*

TABLE OF CONTENTS

Part I

PREPARING YOURSELF FOR BUSINESS OWNERSHIP

Part II

GETTING IT RIGHT THE FIRST TIME:
HOW TO EXAMINE A FRANCHISE

Part I

PREPARING YOURSELF
FOR BUSINESS OWNERSHIP

Introduction

Over the years, I've coached thousands of people who wanted to learn more about opportunities for entrepreneurs in the world of franchising. After working with such a wonderful cross section of people and industries, I saw the need for a well balanced book. You'll gain the greatest value from this book by understanding why it was written and what makes it different from other books about franchising or business entry.

Many books on franchising either try to convince you business ownership is easy, or they state that business ownership is filled with uncertainties, and therefore impossible to accomplish on your own. This book does neither. It is designed to educate you, not to sell you.

The purpose of this book is really quite simple. It is to help you recognize quality franchise opportunities that fit you.

As you look at available franchises, you will find four possible outcomes. You may identify:

1) A successful franchise that matches your skills and objectives.

2) A successful franchise that does not match your skills and objectives.

3) An unsuccessful franchise that matches your skills and objectives.

4) An unsuccessful franchise that does not match your skills and objectives.

It should go without saying the only type of franchise you should move forward with is Option #1 – A successful franchise that matches your skills and objectives.

A secondary purpose of this book is to give you the courage to make the right decision. If the concept is unsuccessful or just wrong for you,

you should have the courage to say no. If the concept is successful and a match to your skills and objectives, you should have the courage to say yes with confidence.

I'll teach you about franchising and equip you with the knowledge you need to properly choose the right course of action. In no way would I imply that franchising or business ownership is for everyone. That is simply not the case.

In order for you to make a great business decision, I'm transferring my experiences as an entrepreneur, teacher, franchisor and franchisee to you.

MY BACKGROUND

My parents immigrated to the United States from Europe in 1963, the year before I was born. They arrived in America with $500 and a single trunk containing all their belongings. Due to my Dad's limited formal education, corporate America was not an option for him, so he quickly focused on business ownership as a better way to provide for his family. My father ended up owning a successful business in Kansas City for more than 35 years. I grew up listening to management issues over the dinner table and watching my father deal with payroll on Monday evenings – payday for employees was Tuesday.

In many ways, my story is typical of many first generation Americans. While my parents never pushed me, the clear pathway was to get a good education and find security in a well-paying job once I graduated. At that time, nobody from my family had graduated from college, and after all, virtually all parents want something better for their children.

After my undergraduate studies, I spent the next seven years working in corporate America. I also spent time teaching and opened a small business for several years.

Eventually I earned an MBA and entered the world of franchising. Over the next decade I held Director and Vice President positions with major franchise brands (Popeye's Chicken and Biscuits®, Church's Chicken®, Cinnabon® and Seattle's Best Coffee®). During my tenure with these brands, I helped develop these concepts in more than 30 countries. I also frequently served as an expert speaker on franchising in numerous countries around the world.

In 2002, having had significant success on the corporate side of franchising, I returned to an entrepreneurial track. I determined my strongest contributions could come from teaching people and helping them analyze business entry. I also knew I wanted the flexibility to spend more time with my wife, children, business and investments.

As a franchise consultant, I've earned a solid reputation as an industry leader and have coached many new business owners to success. While other business interests and investments provide me with passive income, I am passionate about my "active" professional life as a business mentor.

I find it gratifying to share the knowledge in this book with you.

THE BOOK

This book is divided into three parts.

Part I is a grouping of five chapters that will help you build a road map based on your skills and objectives. Ideally you will know enough about yourself to quickly recognize whether a franchise business is worth pursuing.

To begin, you will examine fear and its surprisingly positive role in your decision-making. You will also examine the vital role of vision in business entry and focus on skill-set matching. The final chapter in Part I explores the financial aspects of business ownership.

This is a journey of learning and Part I will give you the framework you need to recognize if an opportunity is right for you.

Once you have concluded your essential self-examination, you'll find great value in the nuts and bolts oriented chapters of Part II. These chapters focus on the method a prospective new business owner should follow in studying specific businesses for possible entry.

Finally, Part III gives you advice about how to increase your prospects for successful business ownership. By focusing on the simple, straightforward advice in this final section, you will find yourself in control of your professional and personal growth as a business owner.

Having both owned businesses and helped others become business owners, I can tell you that building a successful business can be one of the most satisfying acts of your life. This book is designed to help make sure you find the very best business for you.

Chapter 1

Leveraging Your Natural Fear

Courage is resistance to fear,
Mastery of fear -
Not absence of fear.
– Mark Twain

Why start this book with a chapter on fear? What does this have to do with becoming an entrepreneur or buying a franchise? I have chosen to focus on fear because fear is the primary reason most people will never own a business.

It is not a lack of opportunity, it is not your spouse, it is not your children and it is not a lack of ability. It is the fear of failure. This fear of failure can lead to an inability to make a decision and to paralysis with regard to achieving the many goals you may have in life.

Fear is something we have all learned to accept as a part of our lives, but few have actually thought about why, from time to time, we are fearful. It's time to open your eyes to a new way of thinking about fear. It's time to embrace and leverage your fear. I want you to come away from this chapter with both the knowledge and a game plan regarding how you are going to leverage your fear to your advantage.

Fear is not easy to define. It's not even easy to think about. But even for people who appear to be fearless, fear is present. Consider the textbook definitions of fear.

"An emotion experienced in anticipation of some specific pain or danger usually accompanied by a desire to flee or fight."
    Source: WordNet 1.7.1 Copyright © 2001 by Princeton University. All rights reserved.
"Be afraid or feel anxious or apprehensive about a possible or probable situation or event."
    Source: WordNet 1.7.1 Copyright © 2001 by Princeton University. All rights reserved.

"Fear is an unpleasant feeling of perceived risk or danger, real or not."
Source: www.wikipedia.org

One thing we all know is that fear is not something we like to talk about. It is not something we are supposed to be proud of. Society tells us to deny, avoid or minimize fear. Societal norms often say it is not right to admit your fear. If you do admit to being fearful, the first thing people say is, "It's alright, you don't need to be afraid."

I contend a certain amount of fear is a good thing. We have fear because there are things in this world that can hurt us. Fear, by design, helps us avoid those dangers and is exceptionally useful in self preservation.

My advice about fear is to get in touch with your natural fear and leverage it to your advantage. We all have the opportunity to actually leverage our natural fear. Take a moment and think of the awesome power of fear. Now think of the leverage it would create for you to harness that kind of energy, using it to your advantage.

UNDERSTANDING FEAR

In order to move forward, the first thing we need to understand is *why* we have fear. Let me ask this very basic question: Have you ever really thought about fear? As you think about fear, consider these questions: Where does it come from? Why do we have fear?

If you go back to the definition of fear, it is most often connected to a perception, real or imagined, of danger or an anticipation of pain. The most interesting part of fear is most definitions include the words: perception, anticipation and possibility. Fear is connected to what we think *might* happen. Your feelings may or may not have any connection to reality. **In many ways, fear directly relates to a lack of knowledge. It is connected to the unknown.**

Opening a business involves a number of unknowns. A lot of question marks pop up when you have never owned a business before, and these question marks, if left bottled up inside, can lead to a great deal of fear and even paralysis. However, our perception of fear and risk changes as we gain knowledge. The following example describes how knowledge and fear are related:

▶ *Diving head first into fear*

Let's imagine you have never been to a swimming pool with a diving board, but you were told that it is possible to jump off this thing called a high dive. One day you ride your bike to the pool and it is closed. The water is smooth and the high dive is majestically positioned at the side of the pool. Let's imagine you look at the water and the high dive for one hour. At the end of the hour, do you have more fear or less fear? For many people the answer would be more fear. They know how to swim, but they don't know how to dive. They have not learned anything but have had one hour to imagine all the things that could happen. The reality is if you overcame your fear, climbed over the fence and jumped off the high dive with no knowledge of how to do it, there is a relatively high chance you would hurt yourself.

Now let's imagine you return to the pool, watch a number of people jump off the high dive, interview some of them in regard to best practices, speak with the lifeguard regarding number of injuries and calculate the probability of success. You even take a class on how to best enter the water from that height. Now, do you have more fear or less fear? For most people, the answer is less fear. This is because you now have more knowledge. You are not only able to make a better decision regarding whether to jump, but you also have a much better chance of having a successful first jump.

Finally, let's say you have jumped off the high dive 20 times. Do you have more fear or less fear on the 21st jump? Obviously the answer is less fear. Now you not only have knowledge, but you also have experience.

I share this example to make a point. The knowledge and preparation we bring to a situation will dramatically affect both the perception of danger and the actual danger. **Quite simply, an increase in knowledge decreases fear while increasing our potential success.**

WHAT HAPPENS IF . . .

Keeping in mind we will never eliminate fear, I encourage you to embrace and use fear. When you are considering opening a business, you will have a number of uncertainties. Your mind will be running at full speed and a large number of questions will be created. Almost every question will begin with "What happens if…"

- What happens if I go out of business?

- What happens if the franchisor disappears tomorrow?

- What happens if the market changes and there is no need for this service or product?

As you are looking at opening a business and get closer to making a decision, the number of "What happens if" questions will increase. Society tells us to suppress our fear. Society says that we must be strong and brave. I say *use* your feeling of fear to gain knowledge by writing down every question that pops up in your mind, no matter how silly or trivial you think it is, and research it.

If the first 'What happens if' question is, "What happens if I go out of business?" write it down and then dissect the question. What are some related questions you can ask that will give you information and guidance in this area? Try these: "Over the past two years, how many people have gone out of business?" "Why did they go out of business?" "What percentage of the total system has gone out of business?" And so on. Every question can be dissected into a group of additional questions designed to give you more factual information.

Again, the more information you gather, the lower the fear and the higher your likelihood of success. Use your fear to motivate you to get more knowledge. The more fear you have, the more questions you'll ask and the more knowledge you'll gain. This will allow you to get as close as possible to certainty before you make any decisions about entering the business.

IS RISK THE SAME FOR EVERYONE?

Do you believe risk is the same for all people? Does risk exist independent of the person or is it contingent upon the individual? The reality is that risk is *not* the same for all people. It depends on the individual. Buying houses and reselling them is comfortable for some people, but not for others.

Owning a business in and of itself is not particularly risky. The risk comes in when the prospective owner applies their skills and abilities to it.

Everyone begins this journey being "Unconsciously Incompetent." From there you move through the stages of "Consciously Incompetent," "Consciously Competent" and finally, "Unconsciously Competent." The fact is risk and fear are different in each level.

Unconsciously Incompetent – This person has no fear because they have no understanding. Let's use swimming as an example: take a young child who cannot swim. They are likely to walk into the water, and without knowing the risks, walk out too far. That is why we have to be so careful to protect our youngsters around water. Like the child, a first time business owner is at higher risk because they have no, or limited, ability to understand the nature of the action and the possible results.

Consciously Incompetent – At a certain point, the child who hasn't yet had swimming lessons learns that jumping into the water without being able to swim is risky. They try breathing under water once and quickly learn they get water up their nose! They must be more careful. Now they are Consciously Incompetent. There is a lot of uncertainty, and they know they must learn to close their mouth and hold their nose before they jump into the water. The majority of readers of this book are in this stage regarding business ownership. Unfortunately, this is the stage with the most fear. There is a lot that is unknown, and you must gather knowledge to better understand how to move forward.

Consciously Competent – After enough practice, the child is ready to start swimming. This is the point where they start using the knowledge they have gained. The destination is the other side of the pool. Spotters provide a safety net in case they have trouble getting across. They have a well thought out plan based on the success of others. When they make it to the other side of the pool, they are proud of their accomplishment. At this stage of business development, you are more focused on actions than fears. You know you can *swim* in the business pool and you like exercising your newfound skills.

Unconsciously Competent – As the child grows older, they no longer think about how to swim. It just comes naturally. They know water has some risks, a person can drown, but they also know that a swim can be very relaxing and can be a great way to exercise. They are comfortable with the risk and cannot imagine what it must be like not to be able to swim. They are now Unconsciously Competent.

You need to understand that risk is not the same for everyone. Water is not fundamentally risky, just as owning a business is not fundamentally risky. It the way that we interact with the environment, the knowledge we gather and the safety nets that we establish that determine the level of risk.

MIXING FEAR AND THE HUMAN PSYCHE

Fear is an incredibly powerful emotion. Approached properly, fear can be exceptionally helpful.

Many studies have shown that people will react more quickly and with greater commitment when they fear pain or loss than if they desire pleasure or gain.

Let's say, for the sake of example, you're single and you're enjoying a social occasion at a popular local restaurant. Nearby there is someone you are interested in meeting, and you decide you're going to make that happen. Chances are you'll think about it a bit, consider an appropriate way to introduce yourself and maybe even take a break for a mirror check. Unless you're tremendously impulsive, you will put some thought into it.

Now look at the exact same situation, but someone yells, "Fire! Everybody get out of here!" Now, is that person you were interested in meeting before even on your mind as you're clamoring for the door along with the rest of the crowd? That's highly doubtful.

The fear of loss or pain is very powerful, but let's take the example one step further. Let's say after you run outside, you hear a voice from inside the restaurant and you realize there is a person still in the restaurant. They are trapped under a heavy beam that has fallen. What would you do?

When you mix fear and the human psyche you get one of two possible results. The first result is paralysis. Not only can't you decide what to do, but in this type of situation, you may not be able to call for help or even physically move. Fear completely shuts you down.

The other potential result is tremendous power. You immediately rush back into the building despite the significant personal risk; you physically lift the beam and rescue the person. In this case, fear created a massive adrenaline rush and actually allowed you to do things no normal, sane person would ever be able to do.

Fear and the human psyche are a powerful combination. You can use this emotion as a tool to significantly raise your level of play.

FEAR AND SUCCESS

If you study successful business people, you will find they all have fear. Many people believe successful business people are driven by an overwhelming need to succeed. Although this is true with some, it may not be with the majority. **The number one motivator of successful business people is the desire not to fail!** Every day they work hard to make sure they are doing all the things they can to ensure they do not fail. This one emotion – fear – is the most powerful driver of success.

It is well known that Johnny Carson had a lifetime of stage fright. He feared being on stage! As a result, he showed up to work early, extensively prepared for each day's show and focused on what he had to do to make sure the show did not fail that night. He then went on stage. In other words, Johnny Carson harnessed his fear, focused the energy of fear and created one of the most successful late night talk shows in history. Fear can do this for you if you are willing to harness its power.

SUMMARY

If you are going to be successful as a business owner, you must learn how to leverage your fear to create success. It is a powerful force that affects everyone, whether we like to admit it or not. Every decision you make in life has a degree of uncertainty and the possibility of a less than ideal outcome.

As a business owner, you will always be faced with uncertainty. If you are not able to digest the information and make good, timely business decisions, business ownership may be the wrong course for you. If, on the other hand, you are able to harness fear to gain more knowledge, use fear to focus you and master fear to your benefit, you have the potential to be exceptionally successful as a business owner.

Chapter 2

Your Vision

*Shortly after beginning a journey, Alice reaches
a fork in the road and asks the Cheshire Cat:*

"Would you tell me, please, which way I ought to go from here?"
"That depends a good deal on where you want to get to," said the Cat.
"I don't much care where," said Alice.
"Then...it doesn't matter which way you go..." said the Cat.
"...so long as I get SOMEWHERE," Alice quickly added as an explanation.
"Oh, you're sure to do that," said the Cat, "if you only walk long enough."

— Lewis Carroll (*Alice In Wonderland*)

Imagine you're back in the third grade, in a roomful of eight-year-olds, all brimming with curiosity and wonder. The teacher poses these questions to all the students, "What do you want to be when you grow up? And why?"

Now think about the likely responses.

"I want to be a fireman ... to put out fires and make people safe."

"I want to be a doctor ... to save people and make them well."

"I want to be an astronaut ... to explore new worlds."

How often would we hear these answers?

"I want to be an accountant so I can keep the books in order."

"I want to work for IBM so I can have a great health care program and a company car."

"I want to go to an office building every day and have a parking place with my name on it."

In my daily work, I have asked literally thousands of people this question. Amazingly, when I ask people about their visions, I almost always get comments like, "I want a job" or "I want to own a business." So what happened to us as we aged?

The fact is those fresh-thinking kids have a lot better idea of what vision truly is than their adult counterparts. Children, with open minds and clean slates, don't have their future visions spoiled by statistics, spreadsheets, analysis and self-doubt.

Their visions are grander. In their minds, being a lion tamer or mountain climber hasn't been ruled out by financial or physical realities.

Their dreams are more alive. As adults, many of us have replaced vision with short-term goals.

As an example, does this sound like a dream? "I can see us achieving a 12% margin increase next quarter."

Nope. But how about this, "I want to be able to travel the world and visit 25 countries with my spouse."

Now that's *vision!* Why? Because now you have a cornerstone to your future. This vision statement leads to action questions such as, "What do I need to achieve my vision?" The answer is time, money and health. "How much money? Where will I find the time? How late in my life can I wait to begin to make my vision a reality?" These are great questions, but they only get asked if you begin with a vision.

As a prospective entrepreneur, you need to remember that owning your own business is not easy. You will be challenged. Having a clear vision of the future and knowing how the business will help you achieve your vision allows you to greatly increase your ability to work your way through the challenging times.

In this chapter, you begin the entrepreneurial journey with the essential starting point – having a vision and knowing where you're going.

The goals of this chapter are to empower you to:

• Take control of your vision

• Decide where you really want to go

- Determine how you want to get there

- Assure you have a strong belief in your vision

In fact, of those goals the first one is an underlying theme for the entire book: taking control of your own destiny.

IT'S YOUR VISION; TAKE CONTROL OF IT!

When I'm advising individuals or groups about businesses to explore, I ask them what they may be interested in pursuing. Sometimes they'll say something like "I don't know, it depends on the business." In my mind, that amounts to the "tail wagging the dog."

Your vision is up to YOU. It should be you and your vision that determine what business opportunity to select, not the other way around. To say, "it depends on the business," surrenders the power over your own dream and makes it part of someone else's business plan.

So, what is a vision? **A vision is simply an attractive, motivating dream backed by a plan to achieve the dream**. An effective vision creates personal energy and commitment to inspire yourself and those around you. It gives you a backbone of purpose and meaning as you execute your plan; and it helps you bridge today with tomorrow.

Think about a vision as being your destination. It is where you are going. The business (or job) is simply a vehicle to get you there. If you know your destination, it is always easier to choose the best vehicle.

VISION IS ABOUT WHAT YOU WANT
THE FUTURE TO LOOK LIKE

Use that framework for your exploration of entry into the entrepreneurial world.

This is a time when the ball is totally in your court. As you move forward, many of your other decisions will be affected by external factors, some of which are beyond your control.

Forming your vision is something YOU control, so don't shortchange yourself. Whether you see yourself hosting guests at a quaint bed-and-breakfast or traveling the world, it's YOUR vision and YOU must own it.

DECIDE WHERE YOU REALLY WANT TO GO

Look ahead and envision what that future looks like. By doing this, you significantly increase your chances of getting there.

Having worked with thousands of people over the years, I know that creating a personal vision statement is easier for some people than for others. Here is some practical guidance in regard to discovering your personal vision of the future:

A vision statement must clearly outline your projected future. In order to determine your projected future, begin by listing your goals and dreams, regardless of whether they are practical. Questions that can help you in this process include:

- What kind of person do I want to be in the future?

- What do I want people to think of when they see me?

- What do I want to be remembered for?

- What type of legacy would I like to leave behind?

- What is truly important to me?

- What brings me happiness?

- What am I most proud of?

You may also want to list the things you do *not* want in your future:

- What do I not want to be remembered for?

- What do I not want to do during my retirement years?

- What limitations do I want to avoid?

Once you have a handle on what is important to you and what you want to avoid, you need to clearly and concisely draft your personal vision. The vision must be exciting and motivating to you while also respecting your limitations. Don't be afraid to challenge yourself; these are the most satisfying visions to achieve.

For most people, a vision statement takes no more than three to five sentences. The process of refining the vision to a short statement will both clarify and empower the vision, making it practical and useful.

One of my most memorable experiences in career coaching came from listening to the inspiring vision of a couple who were very straight-forward in their response when I asked them where they wanted to be in the future.

Their church and its mission work were very important to them, and they were clear in their intent to be solely focused on their mission work ten years from that date.

They said they wanted to continue to live in their current home, but in the future they intended to spend half of their time traveling abroad as missionaries so that they could help others.

I then asked them if they knew what it would take for them to accomplish those goals and live that particular lifestyle. They proceeded to describe their financial plans for paying for their home and investing to preserve the lifestyle they currently enjoyed.

The clarity of their vision, the commitment with which they described the vision and the definitive timetable for achieving the vision were exceptionally powerful.

In short, that couple was the perfect model for knowing where they wanted to go.

Of course, most people do not have that much clarity. More often, people are generally aware they want to retire comfortably, live in a particular area and have time to spend with the grandchildren. But regardless of the clarity of the future vision, it's important to set that destination and then determine the mileposts that must be achieved in order to get there.

DETERMINE HOW TO GET THERE

Once you are clear about your destination, you must consider the best path to take and how you plan to travel down that path. If you choose correctly, you greatly increase the likelihood of making your vision a reality.

Let's look at it in terms of planning a cross-country trip from Miami to Seattle. Any number of roads and vehicles are available; your choice depends upon your needs. If you're working on a big project at work and can't leave until Friday for your friend's Saturday wedding, the path and vehicle are critical. You must go via the most direct path and you must use the fastest mode of transport. This will mostly likely mean air travel.

Now let's change the scenario. Let's say you have accumulated vacation time and a friend from college has invited you to spend time in Seattle. Let's also say that along the way you'd like to visit friends and relatives in other locales. Suddenly you have more options to consider. You may elect to cruise the state highways on your motorcycle. Your motorcycle trip costs less and you see more of the country. But the trip also takes a lot longer.

Quite simply, the trip will feel very different depending on the path and the vehicle you choose.

The same thought process applies to determining what type of vehicle will get you to your vision. If you're 55 years old and wishing to retire in five years, your needs may be a lot different than the needs of a 25-year-old who is unmarried and wishes to both raise a family and retire by age 50.

So, what vehicles are available to you? Consider these:

- Traditional employment
- Self-employment
- Business ownership
- Investment in real estate and/or equities
- A combination of approaches

▶ *Traditional employment*

Let's say you're employed in a high-level position with a really solid company. At the moment, you're enjoying all the perks normally associated with that type of position, such as substantial bonuses, club memberships, 401k and pension plans.

The questions you need to ask yourself include:

- Am I on track now to achieve all my personal financial benchmarks to attain my vision of the future?

- If not, what advancements will I need to take place in my employment situation? What degree of confidence do I have about being able to achieve these advancements?

- If so, what is my degree of certainty about my long-term employment situation? Is my position stable? Is my company stable? Am I sure my company won't be sold?

- What is my risk profile? If I lose my job at age 55, will I be able to secure another job with the same salary and benefits?

You may be with a fantastic blue chip firm. You may be a top performer, and may not have made any personal monetary investment in your firm.

So you may be inclined to answer the above questions with close to 100% certainty. If that is really the case, congratulations! That is the correct vehicle for you. But keep in mind if you are NOT in control of all the variables, it is impossible to have 100% certainty.

Most people need to consider that as time goes by, a person's employability decreases. Once you are past your primary age of employability, which tends to extend until around fifty-five years old, you will be forced to consider a reduced salary, retirement or other vehicles to achieve your goals.

▶ Self-employment

Many people who suddenly find themselves unemployed – voluntarily or not – consider independent consulting as a possible best option. Many executives become consultants at some point in their lives. People usually become consultants at the following times:

1) Between jobs

2) After their years of employability end

3) When flexibility is of utmost importance

Most professionals believe they have talent and expertise, and chances are they may have a network of contacts still in place from their previous position. Self-employment allows for a low-investment, work-from-home model that translates to a high margin for any revenue they generate. There are also attractive tax advantages in self-employment.

Of course, as with all things, there is a downside. Consulting usually requires more marketing and sales efforts than most people anticipate and the resale value of your "business" is usually non-existent.

Self-employment can provide you with a nice income stream for a period of time, but usually the consultant gets distracted and the independent consulting business eventually shuts down after having served its purpose.

▶ Business ownership

The most significant fact to consider in business ownership is that you are investing in your future and in yourself. This can be intimidating to some. For others, the sense of adventure, control over the future and the potential return are energizing.

Business ownership should, over time, scale to the point where you have employees assisting you with the business. Ideally the work of the business will be done by the employees, whether the business is a franchise, a startup or an existing business. And if your business grows, the resale value should grow steadily, yielding a healthy return when it is time to sell the business.

▶ Investments

Real estate and equities are too often mistaken as businesses. Although some high wealth individuals have turned these into businesses, for the majority of people, these are not businesses—they are investments. It is possible to become a professional investor, once you have sufficient assets to do so. If that is your goal, it makes sense to begin educating yourself now about the fluctuations of the market.

Many people are disappointed when the market stops moving in what they consider the "right" direction. Whether "flipping" houses or day-trading stocks, the investor needs to be cognizant that the markets have always been – and will always be – characterized by self-correcting phenomena. Stocks tend to go up for a while, and then they go down. The same applies to real estate, as well as most other investment approaches.

As a result, it makes the most sense to begin to educate yourself early in regard to investments, realizing you are going to make some mistakes. Stay as involved in your investments as possible. This way you will learn. As your net worth and your knowledge increase, you are more likely to make astute investment decisions, which should lead to a comfortable income stream.

▶ *Combination*

It is important to realize none of these vehicles are mutually exclusive. In fact, it's probably best to look at blending two or more of these strategies into your long-term plans.

Many married couples will have one spouse retain a job for the first 12 months, while the other spouse starts a business. As time goes by and the business is producing a solid cash flow, the first spouse may leave the job and join the business on a part-time basis while also focusing on investments.

My wife and I employ a blend of all of the above strategies, except for employment, which doesn't give us the leverage we need to fully achieve our vision.

The key to success is being clear about your game plan and then having the commitment and consistency to stick to the game plan over the long haul.

BELIEVE IN YOUR VISION

Many people read or hear about vision and dismiss it too quickly. Some of the skepticism associated with vision relates to failed visioning exercises in large, corporate bureaucracies. Perhaps you have been part of a quality team that worked on a vision statement. The result of the team's hard work may have been some coffee mugs and banners, with only lip service to the vision thereafter.

In some cases, skepticism is understandable.

But in the real world of entrepreneurship, *Vision* is spelled with a capital V, because it's necessary, it's genuine and it's practical.

You are the driving force for your future. Nobody else cares whether it happens; only you do. It's your responsibility to create the vision and your responsibility to drive toward it. You must believe in it with all of your heart. Other people did it, and so can you!

There's a compelling thought expressed in the timeless 1937 classic, *Think and Grow Rich*. The author, Napoleon Hill, states:

"Anything the mind of man can conceive of and believe in, it can achieve."

Think about that, beginning with, "Anything the mind of man can conceive of...." Many people think conceiving an idea is the hard part. *How could I possibly conceive of a breakthrough idea? I am not Gates or Ford. I don't know how to conceive of a great idea.*

But to "conceive of" an idea is not the hard part! Any group of reasonably intelligent people in a room together for an afternoon with a flip chart could "conceive of" some pretty good ideas.

On the other hand, some people believe that to "achieve" is the hard part, but that is not the case either. How many times have you seen one company fail at an idea and another succeed? If an idea is achievable, why does this happen? Most of us are good at working hard if we know that we are moving in the right direction.

The real challenge for most people is to "believe in" our visions. For proof, consider the well known Thomas Edison model. Yes, we're amazed he brilliantly came up with the light bulb idea. But how many "failed" experiments did it take to invent the light bulb? Hundreds!

If Edison had not believed in his vision with all his heart and soul, the light bulb would have simply been invented by someone else. When asked to describe his feelings about the failures he had experienced, Edison replied he had merely discovered all the ways NOT to light an incandescent bulb.

Here is a great example of the tremendous importance of belief. Let's examine the computer game called FreeCell. If you haven't played the game, it is similar to solitaire. However, unlike solitaire, all FreeCell games are solvable. Before you move the first card, the game can be won. As you play the game, you either play to a successful conclusion or to where the cards appear unsolvable. The problem with the unsolvable game is you don't know if it is real or perceived. Once you feel the game is unsolvable, you may give it another minute or two, wondering if there is a solution. But more than likely, you will give up after a few minutes and deal a new deck of cards.

An advanced version of the game called FreeCell Pro has a "solver" button. When you are in a jam, you can click on the solver button and it tells you if there is a solution to the game. It does not tell you how to figure out the puzzle, it simply tells you *if* it can be solved. If the answer is solvable, then how long do you think someone will look for a solution? That's right – possibly forever.

When there is belief a solution exists, the level of commitment intensifies. Edison obviously was convinced his puzzle had a solution, so he didn't stop trying. That's why committing to your vision is crucial to your success.

SUMMARY

It all starts with you – and only YOU!

It's not a matter of whether the business market holds opportunities for new entrants. Of course it does, and it always will. And it's not a matter of whether the timing is perfect. After all, there is no such thing as perfect timing for any of our major life-changing decisions. Perfect timing only happens in the movies!

Your vision is something that's uniquely yours. Market forces may be able to dictate some of your financial realities, but regardless of where you are starting, no one can adequately capture or express your vision better than you.

And since you own your vision, take firm control of it; allow it to be big picture, an achievable dream to which you will attach an action plan.

At this point you also need to determine if you want to be an employee, self-employed, a business owner or an investor. One of these pathways is going to be the best vehicle to move you toward your vision.

Then hold on to your vision, investing your passion in it. And when you do, your game plan for achieving your vision has a solid foundation that you can build upon for your entire entrepreneurial journey.

Chapter 3

Essential Traits of an Entrepreneur

Somehow I can't believe that there are any heights that can't be scaled by a man who knows the secrets of making dreams come true. This special secret - curiosity, confidence, courage, and constancy, and the greatest of all is confidence. When you believe in a thing, believe in it all the way, implicitly and unquestionable.
— Walt Disney

You have a clear vision in mind. You know the goal, the destination, and you believe business ownership may be the correct vehicle for you. Now you need to look inside and make a comparison of your traits and how they match up with the essential traits of an entrepreneur.

If you've decided to use entrepreneurship as a vehicle to your dreams, it's time to ask the question, "Am I really cut out to be an entrepreneur?"

I've helped thousands of people make great decisions about business entry. With so many experiences, I've heard all kinds of excuses people have used to justify NOT going into business.

Many people I've talked to will never open their own business. Many people shouldn't. One man I worked with sought advice from his 89-year-old grandmother, who said she thought business entry wasn't a good idea for him. I asked him whether the grandmother had ever owned a business or been around someone who had. The answer was "no."

But this particular individual was looking for an excuse, another way to say, "I don't have what it takes."

It's really OK to come to the conclusion that entrepreneurship isn't for you. In fact, the chances are if there is that much self-doubt, a different choice really would be better.

What does it take to be a successful entrepreneur? Is it some elusive quality that defies description? Actually, it's really not. If you're one of the many people who think there is some mystical quality that only entrepreneurs possess, this chapter is intended to break down the self-destructive barriers that may be holding you back.

In this chapter, I will describe six essential characteristics shared by the majority of successful entrepreneurs:

- Trait #1: Having a clear vision

- Trait #2: Confidently communicating the vision

- Trait #3: Setting a timetable for achievement

- Trait #4: Viewing setbacks as learning opportunities

- Trait #5: Standing apart from the crowd

- Trait #6: Focusing on continual learning

Everyone has some of these traits. The question you have to ask yourself is, "Do I have enough of these traits?"

When you look in the mirror, who do you see, really? How badly do you wish to succeed? Are you willing to stick with the business through the hard times? Will you be able to sleep at night?

Your answers to those and other questions are vital in addressing the central question of whether YOU truly fit the profile of a successful entrepreneur.

Think of three successful people. Who are the people who come to mind when you hear the term *leader* or *successful*? Think of people you admire and would like to pattern yourself after.

Stop your reading and write down the names of these people. As you go through the chapter, use these important people as your measure and see how they match up with the essential traits of an entrepreneur.

Write down the name of:

1) A person in business who has been successful and whom you admire: _____

2) Someone from the world of politics, now or through history, who has demonstrated great leadership: _____

3) Any other person, from any field, who strikes you as a model of leadership and success in business: _____

As you work through this chapter, use these examples and determine what common characteristics they may share. At the same time, consider the degree to which you possess these traits.

TRAIT #1: HAVING A CLEAR VISION – FOR YOURSELF AND YOUR BUSINESS

Do you now have a clear vision? If so, you can use it as a foundation to measure against. Corporate America all too often develops a vision and literally puts it on the shelf. Almost everyone can tell stories about coffee cup slogans being the only reminders of a company's vision or mission statement exercise.

Put vision to work for you, and not just as a tool or an option – but as the foundation of your entire entrepreneurial game plan. The entrepreneur must have a vision; a vision that sets the course for the entire organization and drives everyone toward a mutual goal.

Most leaders have visions of what they want to achieve. Martin Luther King, Jr. had a vision, and he shared it with us in his "I Have a Dream" speech and every speech thereafter. John F. Kennedy had a vision where he saw an American walking on the moon. Bill Gates has a vision with his educational foundation, a vision strong enough to motivate Warren Buffett to donate $37 billion to that cause.

Not all visions are that grand. The couple I mentioned in Chapter 2 wanted to spend time on missionary work. Most people want to have more time to spend with their children and to provide the personal attention that is required to raise them to become happy, well adjusted young adults. Some people want to build a trust for future generations.

There are many visions out there. What is important is that you have a vision and know where you are going. Look back to the three leaders you identified at the beginning of the chapter: Did they have a vision? Did they have clarity in regard to their direction? Did they seem to move with purpose?

TRAIT #2: COMMUNICATING THE VISION
AND MOTIVATING OTHERS TO ACTION

A successful leader and entrepreneur must believe in their vision – AND be prepared to share it with others in order to stimulate confidence throughout the organization. Your first true test is to open your vision up for scrutiny, judgment and criticism.

You may want to start with those closest to you, the people who can be both your friends and your toughest critics. How does your vision sound? Can you share the vision with pride and confidence?

Look back at your list of leaders. Were they willing to share their vision? Were they strong enough to stand in front of a group of people and clearly outline a future direction, stand up to non-believers and press forward?

You may have a model to examine from your own work history. Have you worked really hard for someone else? In most cases, you worked that hard because you believed in what you were doing and felt you were a part of something important. If you've done that, then you know what it's like to believe in a vision. Unfortunately, that was someone else's vision.

Now you need to ask yourself if you can promote that same sort of loyalty and passion among the people you recruit and hire.

TRAIT #3: SETTING A
TIMETABLE FOR ACHIEVEMENT

Setting a timetable means making a commitment to achieve your vision. Mileposts are critical in order for the entrepreneur to know progress is being made.

An awe-inspiring leader shares a glorious vision, and then closes the loop by putting a timetable on it. A timetable is the motivator to achieve the vision.

Let's consider the feat of man going to the moon. We are in awe of visionary people like past President John F. Kennedy. Is it because he was able to conceive of something that had never been done before? Perhaps, to an extent.

The truly amazing part, however, was he set a timetable for his vision. Kennedy said man would walk on the moon by the end of the decade! And it happened!

Entrepreneurs set a timetable and hold themselves and others accountable to the timetable. Their vision is more than wishful thinking; it involves taking concrete steps to actualize the vision.

Seeing the total vision clearly isn't always easy, especially when it takes a long time for goals to be accomplished. In Kennedy's case, he didn't get to see his vision realized. However, because he shared it, we all watched the progress toward the goal and celebrated when the goal was achieved.

It takes perseverance, because the progress isn't always readily apparent. At 10 a.m. on any given Tuesday, it is often hard to tell if you're making progress toward your goal.

A simple example comes from boating. Living on the water, my family and I enjoy leisurely rides in our 24-foot pontoon boat. With an 80 horse power outboard motor, our pontoon is not exactly a Coast Guard cutter. Sometimes, when it's windy and the water becomes a bit choppy, it is hard to tell if we are making progress.

During a typical outing, my daughter's hat flew off and sailed into the water. Before you knew it, that hat was floating farther and farther behind us. Quickly we realized we were moving along at a pretty good clip. So fast, in fact, that we had to reverse course pretty rapidly in order to retrieve the hat. Until we saw the hat land in the water, we couldn't tell how much progress we had actually made.

It's often that way for the entrepreneur. That's why it's important to set timetables. Timetables are just like tossing your hat in the water to see if you're making good progress.

TRAIT #4: VIEWING SETBACKS
AS LEARNING OPPORTUNITIES

If you're driving in an unfamiliar area and you get lost because of bad directions or perhaps a detour, do you just give up and go back home?

If you get lost along the way, you're not going to suspend the trip. You look at the delay as a minor setback and then keep moving forward.

On a recent business trip, I followed my on-line instructions to the letter, but sure enough, my prescribed exit was closed for repair. Was this a setback? Sure. Should I consider reversing course and heading back home? Of course not. I proceeded to the next exit, made a few guesses as I negotiated the back streets, and eventually got back on course.

Business ownership is much the same way. If you try a direct mail marketing program and it doesn't yield the results you planned, does it mean you got into the wrong business or direct mail never works? No, it only means that particular program didn't work, and there could be lots of reasons why. Perhaps the setback was even due to reasons beyond your control.

I once advised a friend to hire a sales rep to address his business development needs. My friend followed my advice and hired someone he thought would be terrific. After a period of time, the new salesperson obviously wasn't working out.

Instead of just throwing in the towel and saying hiring a salesperson isn't the answer, he adjusted his approach and hired another person, who worked out tremendously well. **What my friend did was focus on the solution, not the setback**. Just as I had to plot a new driving course when my exit was blocked, my friend regrouped and got back on course and didn't just give up.

Your steadfast belief in your vision will keep you on track. As I noted earlier, Thomas Edison had hundreds of failures before creating the light bulb.

The entrepreneur sees challenges and even disappointments as points on a continuum and does not allow these to dampen his or her vision. The entrepreneur reacts to a failed attempt by saying, "OK, that didn't work. How can we make it better next time?" A setback represents a step toward the goal, not a reason or excuse to just give up.

TRAIT #5: STANDING APART FROM THE CROWD

Exposing yourself to potential failure is not always easy. In fact, it's hard – really hard.

That's why a true leader must be willing to deal with rejection or being cast out of a group. If you suddenly decided to change direction, give up everything you were doing at the time and become, say, a Buddhist monk, what would people around you say? What would your spouse or partner say? What would your friends and family say? Would they think you'd gone crazy? Probably.

That may be an extreme example, but changes of any kind – in business or in personal life – are often greeted with skepticism, challenges and lack of support. That's because it's easy to just stay the course and do exactly what you're doing now. That's how people know you; they're comfortable with current circumstances, and so are you!

What happens if things don't work out? Well, friends and family all too often will say, "I told you so." And that's a difficult thing to contend with.

If your plans do work out, chances are you can be seen as a leader and be admired. You may even show up on someone's list of heroes. Many will admire you for the risk you took.

The entrepreneur knows about calculated risks and that there is a significant difference between risk and risky.

Are you willing and able to keep pursuing the vision in the face of adversity, doubts or ridicule? If so, that is a huge factor in your favor.

TRAIT #6: FOCUSING ON CONTINUAL LEARNING

Entrepreneur and business coach Brad Sugars was asked, "How do you become a better business coach?" His answer, "You become a better coach with every book you read."

As you contemplate business entry, do **not** think of it as the end game or a solution. It's really only the beginning of tremendous learning and growth. Knowledge creates versatility and improves your decision-making skills. That's why it is critical to view every business experience as a lesson.

My reference to learning is not in the academic sense. It's not necessarily about pursuing advanced degrees or taking accounting courses. When entrepreneurs have accounting issues to address, they often outsource those to skilled professionals.

At the same time, the true entrepreneur will read books and articles in the accounting area. They'll read about how to structure tax advantaged corporations, how to reduce taxes, the role of trusts in protecting wealth and so on. **In other words, the entrepreneur is a lifelong learner, not just someone who racks up degrees as bullet points on a resume.**

For the entrepreneur, personal and professional growth go hand in hand. You have to realize you will never know everything. Acknowledging that fact is the first step to learning.

Here's a way to test that concept, and you can try it with any business owner: Ask the business owner if it was necessary to be an expert in all areas before building their business? When the laughter quiets down, they'll tell you they themselves questioned the gaps in their own knowledge as they entered the entrepreneurial world. And it took ongoing education to build their knowledge and skills in all aspects of the business.

Reading this book is a good first step.

Now, measure what you have read in this chapter against your heroes, your models of leadership. Did they have these characteristics?

Then look at yourself. Do you have these characteristics? Have you have exercised and grown these traits in the past, and are you comfortable exercising these qualities in the future?

Are you willing to reach deep for the "hero inside" and utilize the characteristics we all have within us? The six traits are not the exclusive domain of successful entrepreneurs – we all possess them. It's just a matter of finding out how much of each trait each of us has to leverage.

SUMMARY

Nobody can predict whether or not you will be a successful entrepreneur. What you can do is examine successful people and the techniques they use to create success.

1) Successful people know what they want in the future. They have a carefully crafted vision that allows them to immediately know if a given idea moves them toward or away from their goals and objectives.

2) Successful people are willing to communicate their vision and inspire others to follow it. Translating that vision and motivating people to follow it takes courage.

3) Successful people set timetables for completion of tasks. Setting a deadline provides accountability and is necessary as we benchmark success.

4) Successful people view setbacks as bumps in the road. They quickly recover from the setback and never lose focus of the destination. Learning from your mistakes and keeping your eye on the goal is critical.

5) Successful people are willing to stand apart from the crowd. The successful business person knows once they achieve their goals, the naysayers will turn into supporters.

6) Successful people are lifelong learners. There is no finish line. Whatever benchmarks you set, there will always be more to learn.

Chapter 4

Improving Your Chance
Of Success - Matching Skills

*"If money is your hope for independence, you will never have it.
The only real security that a man can have in this world is a
reserve of knowledge, experience and ability."*
– Henry Ford

You now have a clear vision and you believe you have what it takes to be a successful entrepreneur. So what type of business should you look at? Unfortunately, many people begin to look at companies too soon. Until you examine yourself and your skills, it is impossible to know which direction actually makes the most sense for you.

So what if I told you it is now time for you to start thinking *inside* the box?

The common maxim tells us that better ideas come when you think outside the box.

This chapter makes the case not only for thinking inside the box, but for creating your own box!

This chapter focuses on common errors individuals make in this area and on performing the skill assessment that is essential for anyone who goes into business.

During this skill assessment, you'll learn:

- Why "friendly advice" can be harmful.

- How to bring out and catalog your strongest skills and talents.

- How to use skill-matching to find the right business investment for you.

- Why to think inside your own box.

BEWARE OF FRIENDLY ADVICE!

Seeking out the opinion and advice of friends is a common way to gather ideas for business entry. Typically, people float their ideas about going into business by their close friends and relatives. It is only natural because you trust them and they know you, right? Unfortunately, regardless of how well intentioned your friends may be, the advice is often misguided. Most friends are simply not trained to provide you with the advice that you need to hear.

Most of the time what can go wrong falls into one of two categories:

▶ *Category 1 – Community Based Advice*

The first category of advice I call community based advice. Your friends will say, "Hey, our neighborhood is missing a sandwich shop. You should open a Subway." Or they'll tell you, "We have to drive 20 minutes for a movie. You should get a video rental store."

OK, let's assume the community could use a sandwich shop. Well, what does that have to do with you? What if you simply are not suited to do that particular type of business? What if you dread the thought of managing teen employees, or working evenings or unclogging drains? It is not a good match, is it?

This type of advice places the community's happiness over your happiness! Everyone in the community may want a sandwich store, but you may be ill suited to the daily demands of that kind of business.

▶ *Category 2 – Passion Based Advice*

The second category of advice is passion based advice. You know—"Do what you love!" Your well intended friends and relatives may say, "You love cooking. You should open your own restaurant."

You may love chocolate; in fact, you're known as a real chocoholic. But is that enough reason to open a chocolate store? Do you think there might be more to it than eating chocolate all day? It's not enough to love chocolate, you have to love running a retail confectionary business. If you do not want to work in a retail business everyday, you should not open a retail chocolate store. In the end you will stop eating chocolate but still be stuck with a retail business.

You must first be passionate about owning a business that will require certain levels of time, skill and commitment. As Phillip Lechter states so eloquently in his article, *Passion: Friend or Foe*, "Passion is more about what you are being – a business owner, than what you are doing – laundry."

▶ *Jim's Story*

Let's look at a real-life example, a friend from a past work experience:

Jim was a high-level, highly successful sales person at a major corporation, a guy who had been doing major deals all over the world, enjoying some of the fantastic perks that come with that level of achievement. After twenty years, Jim had grown weary of the travel demands and felt ready for a new challenge, a different direction in his life.

He was financially positioned to go into business for himself, so he pondered what might be best for him. One thing was certain, he wanted something different than what he'd been doing.

Jim had a consuming passion for golf. As a by-product of his tremendous success in sales, he had developed a fantastic golf game and had played on some of the greatest courses all over the world. He loved golf!

So at the urging of his well-meaning friends, he directed his sights to a golf business. He decided a golf shop franchise would be the perfect match for him. His dreamy-eyed vision included a life immersed in the golf world.

The problem – he got just what he wished for!

He bought a retail golf shop and opened for business. And before long, what was he doing? He was immersed in golf, alright, but not in the way he had envisioned. He was counting boxes of golf balls, filling in for employees who didn't show up for work and he was getting no enjoyment out of golf or out of the business. In addition, Jim was playing fewer rounds of golf than he did as a sales rep.

Jim had become a person who felt trapped figuratively and even literally. Jim was a person who was accustomed to being on the move. Being confined to a single location every day didn't bring out the best in him. He felt caged.

Needing to break out of the cage, Jim took steps to relieve that anxiety. He hired a general manager to work in the business. Jim got out into the community to do some networking. He tried to get back to the life he once knew. Jim played more golf and convinced himself, as he spent more time out of the business, that he was delegating responsibility to the manager.

Delegating, of course, is a good thing. But yielding full operational control to the manager may be quite another. The risk of completely relinquishing control, with no one managing the manager, is that the manager may not be running the business the way it should be run. When that happens, quality and sales can begin to slip.

Or, as in Jim's case, the manager simply walks out the door one day.

Then, sadly, Jim, the golf enthusiast, became a disenchanted owner who wanted to sell his business.

Someone else came along, someone who used to manage a Target. The owner knew how to manage inventory, knew about managing staff and knew nothing about golf. But he turned the business into a success.

If Jim had looked at what it was that really delighted him professionally – hunting for great prospects, closing big deals, having lots of movement and activity – he would have pursued something dramatically different. He would have looked past the topic of golf, and realized that any retail business which kept him in one place, doing tasks he didn't enjoy, was not a good fit.

What is the moral of Jim's story? He made a series of fundamental errors he could have corrected by doing an honest assessment of his own skills.

A hunter in a farmer's business: Jim liked to get deals done. He liked "the thrill of the chase." But that was not the nature of the golf store business.

His natural habitat: Jim was a very proactive guy who liked to go out into the field and "hunt." In the golf store, he was confined to a stationary situation.

No possibility of satisfaction: The golf store was a business with a lot of small sales. This was not at all what Jim was accustomed to or needed.

No connection to his natural skills: Jim was a guy highly skilled in sales, but the golf outlet took him out of that environment.

Wrong time and place: Jim's dream business did not allow him to play golf. His peak selling hours were now at the times when everyone else, including his friends, focused on playing golf.

It's time to think about opportunity identification in a different way. Time to think about your needs and desires in a different way.

CATALOGING YOUR SKILLS

So what should you do to avoid the fundamental errors Jim made?

<u>**Step 1**</u> - Determine what skills you bring to the table, either independently or with an advisor. You can do this by making a list of the jobs you have held and your responsibilities. Have you managed people, organized things, sold, marketed, analyzed financial data or made presentations? Make sure it's a thorough, honest, skill-set assessment that digs deep.

<u>**Step 2**</u> - List all the functional areas of business and determine where you have strengths and where you do not. Just scratching the surface with an observation like, "I'm a people person," won't cut it. You need to carefully examine each area. One functional area would be sales. Do you have sales skills? If yes, what type of sales skills? Do you have experience with internal or external sales? What type of sales environment would give you the highest chance of success and would challenge you? Do this for each functional area of business.

<u>**Step 3**</u> – List this information together on a single piece of paper.

The good news for you is no business owner can, or wants to, do it all. Successful entrepreneurs make sure to leverage their skills and talents and delegate the other areas. As you are looking at businesses, it only makes sense for you to leverage your skills to the greatest degree possible and supplement yourself in the areas where you may be weaker.

Many times I've witnessed how people from widely divergent industries can achieve great success in the same business. That's because they recognize the skills required and know that the business is a match to their skills.

MATCHING SKILLS AND ACHIEVING SUCCESS

Now that you've armed yourself with a detailed skills assessment, review your vision statement. The skills assessment assures you have the skills; your vision gives you direction and guidelines. If you desire to have flexibility to spend time with your children on weekends and during the evening, add these criteria to your assessment. Make sure that any business you investigate is a good match at all levels. Let these criteria be your guide as you now identify the type of business that is right for you.

At this point you need to target businesses and industries that match both your skills and your vision. You need to conduct this research regardless of industry. Most of us have preconceived ideas regarding industries; it is important to try to eliminate preconceptions. If you want to be "happy," your business has to connect with your skills and your vision.

Volumes of research support the idea that matching skills to work requirements is the key variable of workplace or professional happiness. If people are doing work that matches their skills, they will conduct the work more effectively. If it is done more effectively, people will appreciate the work and ask them to do more. The more work they do, the more positive reinforcement they will receive and the greater the success of the business.

It's a cycle that drives business success – and happiness.

BUILDING YOUR OWN BOX

I mentioned at the beginning of this chapter that you will need to "build your own box." That is what you are doing when you conduct your skill set assessment.

When it comes to business ownership, you can open any type of business. There are no rules in this regard. However, you are not ideally suited to just any business. Just as you are better suited to some jobs, you are also better suited to some businesses. It is critical to build your box carefully and then analyze each business opportunity in regard to whether it is a good match to your skills and your vision.

How do you do this? **Simply ask yourself, "Would I hire myself to manage this business?"** Go through your skills and your vision and see if the argument is strong for you being able to successfully drive the business.

Another question you may ask yourself is, "Even if I have no passion for the product or service, will I still be able to run the business effectively and competently?"

Let's return to Jim the Golfer. Jim was obviously a bad match for a golf store, but what would he be a good match for? Well, Jim's skill set could be ideal for operating a temporary employment services company. That type of business is a great match for the person who likes to "hunt" and succeeds by building relationships. In addition, Jim would likely be able to play a lot of golf while entertaining clients. And we know he certainly likes to play golf and that he didn't get to do much of that in his golf retail business!

That's what I mean by thinking inside the box. A box you build for yourself!

SUMMARY

Make sure you end up with a business that will give you the highest chance of success. Not the one your neighbor suggests or the one you happen to have an emotional attachment to, but the one that will give you the highest opportunity of success and happiness.

It is all about building your own box and then thinking inside your box.

You will need to build a comprehensive profile of your current skills and define each skill with as much detail as you can. You will also need to bring your vision back into the equation to make sure any business you review will match your long term goals. In essence, you are building your own box to make sure that any business you review will match you.

Remember, in the end you will own a "business." You will not own a "golf business" or a "chocolate business" or a "fitness business." You will own a business with core skill requirements. Match your skill and ability to the business model and you will greatly improve your chance for success and happiness.

Chapter 5

Why Own A Business When I Can Get A Job?

Two roads diverged in a wood, and I ...
I took the one less traveled by,
And that has made all the difference.
– Robert Frost

It's one of the most common questions that people ask as they think about whether to go into business.

Many prospective entrepreneurs come from a corporate background, and corporate America does not teach or promote the concepts of ownership or entrepreneurship. In fact, corporations want to shield their most valuable assets, their people, because companies strive to retain valuable employees.

Corporations love to talk to their employees about the value of company cars, club memberships and health care packages, but they're not going to talk to you about the value of owning a business.

As I've worked with people over the years, I regularly see the red flags that signal corporate employee mentality. As we open the discussion of what they want to get out of business ownership, they'll say things like:

"I need a salary of $100,000."

"I want a business where I can pay myself immediately."

When I hear those comments, I know they have not been educated about the concept of ownership. It's time now to examine the mentality of business owners and *why* people own businesses.

We'll examine the logic of business ownership as an asset creation model. As you look at the side-by-side employee vs. business owner comparison, you'll need to shift to a new paradigm, particularly if your only professional history is in a corporate setting as a salaried employee. The way you view the expression of "how much do you make" must change in order to understand the asset building model.

OWNER VS. EMPLOYEE MENTALITY

The argument for ownership over employee status is similar to the case for owning versus renting your home. The great American dream, of course, is to own your own home. Why? Not just for the perceived security of it, although the psychology is understandable, but the stronger, more logical, reason: you're growing an asset that ultimately works for you.

Do you own a home? If you're considering business ownership, the chances are likely you do. So think about your home ownership for a moment. What are the advantages of owning your home? The most common responses to that question include:

- I'm not going to just hand over my money for someone else's benefit every month.

- I want something that belongs to me and can be passed along to the next generation.

- If my home is paid for, I'll always have a place to live.

- I want to invest in something that will appreciate in value.

And that final point is what brings me to the underlying theme of the case for business ownership as the American Dream, Part II— owning a business and creating wealth.

Conversely, entitlement is the underlying concept of being an employee.

In the employer/employee relationship, there is an element of gifting involved. Employees look forward to bonus awards as rewards for their hard work and dedication to the employer. That mentality is pervasive. But what happens if the bonus isn't there, or isn't as large as one had hoped? Things can get pretty ugly if the expected sizable payout isn't given at the end of the first quarter.

If you've been an employee in a company of any size, think of situations in which you questioned why something was being done. You did it because it was mandated by the owner. In such situations, the owner was probably thinking in an asset-building context, while your mind was fixed in the context of getting more and better resources for your division.

For employees, the inclination is to seek resources that will make things operate more smoothly and make work conditions more pleasing. Owners employ a broader vision and understand that sacrifice has to be made in the short run in order to build an asset and achieve greater security in the long run.

Let's look at home ownership again. One often must forgo immediate gratification in order to buy a house. That is what my parents did when they looked at owning their first home after immigrating to America. They had lived here for about 18 months, and my mother was homesick and longed for a visit back home. My father came to my mother and posed this situation to her, "We've saved a little bit of money, and we have a choice to make. We can put the money down on a home, or you can go back to Europe for the summer. What would you like to do?"

They couldn't do both. They had to choose between investing in asset creation or addressing an immediate psychological need. They elected to go back to Europe, and consequently their investment in a home was postponed. That was the tradeoff. They recognized the tradeoff and had to live with that decision.

It is likely that we have to forgo some level of gratification to buy a house. Then, when the house is purchased, additional sacrifices and investments are required. You have maintenance issues, you have tax issues, you have insurance issues—a whole range of expenses we willingly incur because we know owning a home can create value.

That's the same mentality you must have when you look at investing in a business and that is why most people who own businesses generally also own their homes. If asset creation isn't a compelling objective, then having a job is just fine.

THE CASE FOR OWNERSHIP: WHO REALLY MAKES MORE MONEY?

The following example demonstrates the relative differences between business ownership and a job. Let's compare three years as a business owner versus the same time as an employee. The objective of this example is to open your eyes to the relative give-and-take of each approach. It will also help you understand both how business owners think and how to explore wealth creation.

The accompanying charts illustrate the case. Let's study the comparison of a startup business in the first three years to a six-figure corporate job over the same time period. It is The Entrepreneur vs. The Employee.

▶ *Year 1*

	Entrepreneur	Employee
Startup investment	$150,000	$0
Year 1	$200,000 Gross 10% Net $20,000 Owner Benefit	$100,000 salary

At the start of Year 1, The Entrepreneur invests $150,000 to launch the new business. For the purpose of this case study, the source of the startup funds is not relevant. The investment capital could come from home equity, a 401K rollover, a bank loan or a relative. All we need to know is that $150,000 is invested.

Meanwhile, The Employee invests nothing, incurring no debt or risk. If anything, The Employee invested a bit of time and copier expense in preparing a good resume.

Over the course of the first year, let's see what benefits the two of them realized:

In the first year The Employee has a pretty big advantage in terms of income, with a salary that clearly exceeds the $20,000 owner benefit The Entrepreneur takes from the business. In Year 1 there is no arguing the fact a six-figure salary, even after taxes, exceeds the $20,000 owner benefit by quite a margin. The Entrepreneur must be willing to accept this, just as a homeowner accepts the fact he has higher expenses in the first year than the renter.

Of course, many people would discuss the intangible benefits. The business owner, even in a challenging first year, gains an appreciation of the freedom and pride associated with controlling his own destiny. A franchisee I coached reported with satisfaction that he was playing a lot less golf than he did during his corporate career. He proudly stated it was his choice.

Intangibles are not enough to make the case for ownership. Although they are important influences on the emotional side of the ledger, they do not explain wealth creation. On the logical, practical side, it is important to take note of the dollars-and-cents trends taking shape.

For example, the tax ramifications yield a different picture. Owner benefit is worth more than you would expect because of how you are taxed. When The Entrepreneur decides to buy a $30,000 car, it can be purchased directly as a business expense and comes straight out of the business. For The Employee, buying the same car requires more salary dollars, probably $40,000 or more, because earnings are taxed first.

The same would apply to expenses like daycare. The Entrepreneur may incur $5,000 in daycare expense, and it is covered directly by the business because it is an allowed deduction. Once again, The Employee has to earn somewhere around $8,000 to pay for the same amount of daycare because of the tax implications. In the end it just makes sense to pay for things with pretax dollars if you are legally eligible to do so.

One thing many people don't realize is the government actually wants to stimulate the health of small business and offers many tax advantages toward that goal. Advantages that are not only legal and permissible, but strongly encouraged.

Again, this view is not intended to suggest The Entrepreneur's Year 1 owner benefit is equal to or better than the six-figure salary. The point of this comparison is that you have to look at how dollars work.

As you consider business ownership, you may say, "I want to make a $100,000 salary." Actually, what you want to make is the owner benefit **equivalent to** the buying power of a six-figure salary.

► **Year 2**

	Entrepreneur	Employee
Startup investment	$150,000	$0
Year 1	$200,000 Gross 10% Net $20,000 Owner Benefit	$100,000 salary
Year 2	$350,000 Gross 15% Net $52,500 Owner Benefit	$105,000

In Year 2, things improve for both The Entrepreneur and The Employee. The Employee received a very nice raise of 5%, and now has a salary of $105,000 annually.

Meanwhile, The Entrepreneur has done better in the business. His gross revenues have increased from $200,000 to $350,000 and his net income percentage has increased from 10% to 15%—but look at what has happened to his owner benefit. Because of the healthy boost of gross revenues and greater efficiency, owner benefit has now more than doubled from Year 1 from $20,000 to $52,500.

Still, The Employee has an advantage in take-home dollars, but The Entrepreneur is building a business. He has more than doubled the owner benefit and is building the foundation for future growth.

At this point, someone may point out companies furnish great benefit packages for their employees, pointing to 401K and medical insurance packages. Those are nice benefits, but are those benefits only available through large corporations? Of course not!

In a typical corporate 401K program, the company generously matches up to, say, 8% of the employee's contribution. The employee's contribution is typically capped at a certain level as well. While that may seem very generous of the corporation, The Entrepreneur isn't bound by those limits. As an independent business owner, you can drive a lot more money into your retirement program because you are able to determine the way your program is set up. In one year, I protected more than 100% of my salary through the establishment of various retirement programs!

That's the beauty of owner benefit. The owner decides what to do with that benefit – reinvest it in the business, pay down debt with it or use it for personal expenses.

Speaking of significant personal expenses, health care expense is always a major priority for any household. In corporations today, health care is certainly the subject of much discussion. Companies are requiring their employees to spend more on health care, and we're definitely seeing a trend toward health care programs with higher deductibles. Yet many people worry about finding affordable health care insurance and assume large group plans with large corporations are the only safe havens for quality health insurance benefits.

Entrepreneurs are discovering high-deductible plans that are affordable, offer good coverage for catastrophic events and have great tax advantages, either as plans offered by the company or as personal plans that are tax-deductible. Group insurance plans are not exclusively for large companies, as a group can be defined as two or more employees in a company.

Along those lines, take a glance at the healthy trend for The Entrepreneur in Year 2 and keep an eye on the percentage increase in owner benefit line as we continue to Year 3.

▶ *Year 3*

	Entrepreneur	Employee
Startup investment	$150,000	$0
Year 1	$200,000 Gross 10% Net $20,000 Owner Benefit	$100,000 salary
Year 2	$350,000 Gross 15% Net $52,500 Owner Benefit	$105,000 salary
Year 3	$450,000 Gross 20% Net $90,000 Owner Benefit	$108,000 salary

Once again, The Employee was a good employee and was rewarded with another salary increase. His $108,000 pre-tax gross salary exceeds The

Entrepreneur's owner benefit. But the gap is narrowing. In two years The Entrepreneur has gone from $20,000 to $90,000 in Owner Benefit. Who achieved the greater hike in earnings? The Entrepreneur again.

In terms of take-home dollars, The Entrepreneur has at least evened the score, and possibly surpassed The Employee in regard to after tax, net purchasing power.

CREATION OF AN ASSET

This brings us to the most salient point of this entire exercise. Let's compare the asset value The Entrepreneur has created versus the asset value of The Employee's job.

	Entrepreneur	Employee
Startup investment	$150,000	$0
Year 1	$200,000 Gross 10% Net $20,000 Owner Benefit	$100,000 salary
Year 2	$350,000 Gross 15% Net $52,500 Owner Benefit	$105,000 salary
Year 3	$450,000 Gross 20% Net $90,000 Owner Benefit	$108,000 salary
Owner's Business	**+/- $270,000**	**$0**

The Employee's job has an asset value of ZERO! Think about it. Does an employee *own* a job? No. Does an employee own their office or work station? Someone else owns these assets—the business owner!

Speaking of our entrepreneur, look at what happened to the market value of the asset that was created with a $150,000 investment. Because The Entrepreneur worked hard and created a successful business, he can now sell the business if he wishes.

What is the value of this business? It is hard to say, but a reasonable rule of thumb is 3 to 3.5 X owner's discretionary profit (or owner benefit). In this situation, the business would probably be worth around $250,000 to $300,000.

Valuation of existing businesses can be performed in a number of ways, with various criteria, including multiples of cash flow. It is likely the positive growth trend and the positive cash flow of this business in our case study would be quite attractive to prospective business buyers.

WEALTH CREATION

In the end, asset building is about wealth creation. It is about increasing your net worth. At the start of the exercise, the $150,000 investment seemed like a significant setback for The Entrepreneur, while The Employee enjoyed the comfort and ease of settling into a new office to work for a steady paycheck.

Within three years The Entrepreneur had built both cash flow and asset value that exceeded The Employee. This is just the start of the story. Now The Entrepreneur can begin to leverage growth. In the third year The Entrepreneur opens a second location, and in the sixth year he opens a third store. At the end of ten years, all three locations are stable and well established. What has The Entrepreneur created? **How about a cash flow of more than $250,000/year, and more importantly, a business that is worth almost a million dollars!**

This is how wealth is created in a free market economy. Someone invests their capital and builds something of value. That thing of value is desired by others and the value of the item goes up. As the value goes up, the individual becomes wealthy. If you don't believe me, research almost any multi-millionaire. As a matter of fact, start with the billionaires. Bill Gates' salary is less than $1 million per year. How did he amass a $42 billion dollar net worth? He created something of value called Microsoft.

There is an entire book on the subject of wealth creation called *The Millionaire Next Door* by Thomas J. Stanley, PhD, and William D. Danko, PhD. The majority of millionaires in the United States are millionaires due to the businesses they built, not because of the salaries they earned. They state, "In America, fewer than one in five households, or about 18%, is headed by a self-employed business owner or professional. **But these self-employed people are four times more likely to be millionaires than those who work for others."**

If part of your vision is to build a significant net worth, allowing you the freedom to pursue the other things in life that are important to you, then business ownership is a path to seriously consider.

SUMMARY

Making the leap from employee to owner involves two dramatic shifts in your thinking:

1) Shift from the "salary mentality" of an employee to the "cash flow and asset creation mentality" of an owner.

2) Your technical analysis of how much you make must be based on the complete picture of costs and benefits.

All employees, whether front-line or CEO, sell their labor and skills to the owner of the business. The owner, in turn, rewards employees with compensation. No matter how high on the organizational chart, employees are essentially renting their time and skills to an owner. The owner is using the work and skills of the employee to build something of value that the owner can then grow and/or sell.

An employee has very little financial risk in this equation. The major risk is the ability to retain the job and make future income. The employee does not risk their savings in a traditional employee/employer relationship. As you would expect, low risk generally limits your upside potential.

Owners take on more risk. They invest savings to create a business and risk the business not performing to the level they expect. But the owner also derives the majority of the benefit should the enterprise prove to be successful. Once the business is established, they gain security of cash flow, tax benefits and asset creation.

Even though this is a basic risk/reward equation, it is the very foundation of wealth creation in a free market economy.

Part II

**GETTING IT RIGHT THE FIRST TIME:
HOW TO EXAMINE A FRANCHISE**

Introduction

With the completion of Part I, it is likely you now have a clear idea of who you are and what you want out of a business. Part II of this book is all about franchising.

FRANCHISING IN THE UNITED STATES TODAY

Consider this information from the recently completed study entitled "The Economic Impact of Franchised Businesses in the United States" compiled by the National Economic Consulting Practice of PriceWaterhouseCoopers:

Franchised businesses operated 767,483 establishments in the United States in 2001. They provided 9,797,117 jobs, met $229.1 billion payroll and produced $624.6 billion of output. To indicate the economic size in a different way, franchised businesses employed about the same number of people in 2001 as did all manufacturers of durable goods, such as computers, cars, trucks, planes, communications equipment, primary metals, wood products and instruments.

On the scope of franchising, here is more from a study entitled "The Profile of Franchising 2006," produced by FranData:

There were 2,471 franchise systems confirmed active at some point in the five year period 2002 – 2006 with at least one operating franchised unit. Of all concepts, 32% had more than 100 units, 46% had more than 50 units and 25% had less than 10 units.

This data underscores the obvious; franchising is much more than fast food. Today you can find franchised concepts in 75 to 100 different industries ranging from paper shredding to business coaching. Some of these concepts are strong companies that have stood and will continue to stand the test of time. Other concepts leave a lot to be desired and frankly should be avoided. You need to be able to tell the difference between the two.

For more information on the size and scope of franchising, please go to www.educatedfranchisee.com.

CONTENT OF PART II

It will be quite detailed on the subject of how to analyze a franchise. To properly research a franchise (or any business opportunity for that matter), it takes a focused effort.

This chapter begins with foundational knowledge such as:

- What is franchising?
- Where did it come from?
- What do you buy when you buy a franchise?

Detailed explanations, tips, and advice regarding the Franchise Disclosure Document are provided. I also discuss ways to identify high quality franchise systems, how to interview franchisors and franchisees, the right questions to ask to build an effective P&L statement, how to secure financing and how to choose advisors.

In short, there is a lot of information in Part II. Every bit of information in these chapters will be exceptionally useful in helping you conduct a thorough, rewarding business exploration.

Although this is obviously a serious endeavor, I also urge you to have some fun. Always remember, if you do choose to move forward into a franchised business, the franchisor is going to be a type of business partner. Due diligence is critical, but always remember you are also building a relationship. In the end, both parties need to like each other and there has to be a mutual interest in moving forward into a business relationship. So get to know the franchisors, the franchisees, and have fun.

Chapter 6

Foundational Knowledge - What Is Franchising And Where Did It Come From?

Strength does not come from physical capacity.
It comes from an indomitable will.
– Mahatma Gandhi

The next three chapters provide you with the foundation you need to realistically understand franchising.

In this chapter, we'll examine:

- What you actually purchase when you buy a franchise

- Franchising's history and its impact in the U.S. economy

- The strengths and the restrictions of franchising

IS FRANCHISING AN INDUSTRY?

Sometimes stories in the press say, "The franchising industry is really exploding." Or, "Today we report some interesting statistics on the franchising industry." I regularly give presentations on franchising and I often ask the audience "Is franchising an industry?" The majority of educated business people in the audience usually say, "Yes, it is an industry." In fact, even the U.S. Dept. of Commerce categorizes franchising as an industry.

Franchising is **not** an industry. Instead, franchising is more properly categorized as a model for doing business. It is comparable to other ways of going into business, such as licensing, agency agreements, distribution agreements, joint venture agreements or company owned development. People do not typically view those business models as industries, and franchising should not be seen as an industry either.

Take a look at the huge number of industries found within franchising. Is McDonald's® in the franchising industry? I think most would agree that although McDonald's offers franchises, it is clearly in the restaurant industry.

Another example is Starbucks®. Is Starbucks in the franchising industry? The fact is, Starbucks is in the restaurant industry or maybe the coffee industry. They are definitely not in the franchising industry. As a matter of fact, the Starbucks website clearly states they do not offer franchises. The majority of Starbucks in the United States are company owned; they are a chain store. They also have a number of joint ventures and a few licensing agreements, but they have chosen not to offer franchises.

The International Franchise Association defines franchising in their Economic Impact Study in a very clear and concise manner: "Franchising is not a business or an industry, but it is a method used by businesses for the marketing and distribution of their products or services."

SO WHAT DOES THE FRANCHISEE PURCHASE?

Some people may think of buying a franchise as buying a brand name, but the franchisee never owns the brand name. The franchisee simply buys "the right to use the system."

The franchisor has worked hard to perfect a system that can be replicated by others, so what the franchisee is buying is a license to use the system, not the system itself. In the due diligence phase of a franchise investigation, you will find out about the quality of the system. The system may include the right to use trademarks and logos, but you're not buying them.

This is true with all sizes of franchise systems. They are giving you the right to use their system of doing business. Of course, this raises an interesting point: What should you be investigating if you investigate a franchise? Should you be investigating the color of the logo? No, what you should be focusing your research on is the overall quality of *the system of doing business*. Does the existing methodology of doing business improve your chance of success? If the answer is "Yes," then you are probably on to something. If the answer is "No," then walk away.

This lesson also applies after you become a franchisee. You have purchased the right to use the system and you know the system is where the value is found, so what is the first thing you should do after becoming a franchisee? The correct answer is: *follow the system*. This may seem basic, but everyone who enters a franchise system eventually tries to change the system. It is human nature. Try to resist doing it. The system is where the value is found. Leverage your investment by following the system and growing your business.

As you look at alternatives, don't be confused by "business opportunities." Often you can find these on the same websites as franchises. They typically involve selling somebody else's product for them. The seller may provide a training kit that advises how to sell the product, but commonly you're obligated to buy an inventory of products and then bear the obligation to turn a profit from selling them. They are not selling you a system of success but the right to sell their product. These types of operations are not required to follow Federal Trade Commission guidelines as they relate to producing and sharing a Franchise Disclosure Document with all prospective business owners. Both franchisors and franchisees are protected by the Franchise Disclosure Document. The Disclosure Document details the history and financial standing of a company, and it serves as an incredibly useful tool in your evaluation of a franchise. We will cover this in great detail in the next chapter.

If you find yourself reading or listening to a pitch and cannot distinguish whether it is a franchise or a business opportunity, just ask to see the Franchise Disclosure Document. No Franchise Disclosure Document – no franchise. It's that simple.

THE ROOTS OF FRANCHISING

To put franchising in perspective, we'll take a quick look at its early history. As with most things, opinions vary on franchise history, but many would agree franchising originated in medieval times. A sovereign power, a king, queen, church or local government, would grant a franchise to do something such as hunting, organizing events or even collecting taxes. The sovereign power would grant a monopoly and in return, the franchisee would pay a royalty for the monopoly. In this simple form, franchising simply offered an individual or group the "right or privilege" to do something.

Today, this type of franchising still exists all around us. Local governments issue franchises for cable service, gas service, airport usage and mineral deposits on government land. Even my little community in Florida issues a franchise to run a business on the city pier, and the franchise that controls this prime location pays the city a royalty for this monopolistic right.

In the 1890s, franchising evolved and split. Although the old type of franchising still existed (and does to this day), a new type of franchising was created—Business Format Franchising. The first business format franchise was Harper's Beauty Shop, with more than 500 locations throughout the United States, Canada and Europe. Business format franchising is our focus in this book. Business format franchising is a right or a privilege with an operating system wrapped around it.

In other words, if I give you the right to hunt or fish on my land, you have a franchise. If I give you the same right and then provide you with guidance on what type of bait to use, when to check the traps, where to place the traps, how to best clean the pelts – then you have a business format franchise. In this business category, you expect the franchisor will provide manuals and guidance to franchisees about how to effectively operate the system. It is further expected the franchisor will innovate and invest in research and development of both products and services.

GROWTH OF FRANCHISING

Obviously, many books, websites and studies cover this topic.

The 2004 Economic Impact of Franchised Businesses study by the International Franchising Association (IFA) and PriceWaterhouseCoopers, showed franchised businesses accounted for 7.4% of all private sector jobs, 5.0% of all private sector payrolls and 3.9% of all private sector output.

Franchising's total impact on the economy is well beyond the above mentioned numbers, with more than 18 million jobs (13.7% of all private sector jobs) and $506.6 billion of payroll (11.1% of all private-sector payroll in 2001).

Franchising is a powerful force in today's economy. What follows are some of the key reasons why franchising is controlling an increasingly impressive share of the United States economy.

STRENGTHS OF FRANCHISING

▶ *Proven systems*

The following formula explains why so many people explore franchising:

- Proven Systems = Fewer Mistakes

If you find a proven system and then you follow that system, you'll have a much higher chance of success. And your prospects are greater for rapid, significant cash flow.

Everyone wants a higher degree of certainty about short-term and long-term financial success. But the focus on minimizing risk is even more important to people who come from executive careers with large corporations. These individuals tend to be more risk adverse.

That is why systematic due diligence, including a review of the franchisor's Franchise Disclosure Document (see Chapter 7) and a well conducted validation process with existing franchisees (see Chapter 10) are so important. While there are no guarantees for success in any business, only franchising allows the prospective owner to obtain a wealth of information in order to ascertain best prospects for success.

▶ *Expert advice and support*

Another factor that resonates strongly with former corporate employees is the presence of expert advisors in key leadership positions with many franchises. For example, the new franchisee may know nothing about making delicious ice cream, but at the core of the franchise is likely to be someone who perfected a fantastic recipe, and then surrounded himself with experts in preparing and distributing the product.

As you examine the profile of a franchise company, you'll find it important to look at the backgrounds of the key players. If you're buying into a tutoring franchise, for example, you will likely find it more encouraging to discover the direct involvement of skilled educators in key leadership positions.

A great franchise will also have extensive training and support systems designed to get you through the learning curve as fast and as successfully as possible. They will be very organized in how the training and support will happen, in which order and how long it should take.

▶ *Marketing and purchasing power*

Leverage is the name of the game in the many franchise systems, and nowhere is it more evident than in the level of support the franchisor can provide in terms of marketing and procurement.

The marketing power of a collective has the same advantages as a business with a dozen locations in a market. The collective is significantly more efficient than a stand-alone business. Professional marketing materials are expensive and valuable, so having materials provided by the franchisor is a key resource that works to your advantage.

For example, Joe's Pizza, a stand-alone shop, typically will have food photography and other marketing materials that have a lower quality look than the larger operator that paid for high quality materials. The reason is obviously the economy of scale that the larger operation leverages.

At food franchises I worked with in the past, $20,000 might be the budgeted amount for the food photography of a single brochure – that is for six photos! And when that brochure is published, the food is perfect. It actually makes the customer's mouth water. That is powerful.

At the same time, the average stand-alone restaurant cannot afford this type of expense. Joe's Pizza may have a $20,000 marketing budget for the entire year. With that $20,000 Joe has to be careful about his spending. Economically, it's impossible for the stand-alone operation to utilize leverage at the level of a franchise.

The purchasing power of a franchisor, particularly a large franchisor, is especially significant for those who are looking at businesses that require a consumable product. Who do you suppose gets a better price on chicken, Popeye's Chicken and Biscuits or Chuck's Chicken Shack? Who gets a better price on signage, Great Clips® hair salon with 2,500 locations or Sam's Snip and Clip? Wal-Mart® has proven without a doubt that size matters when it comes to purchasing. A mom-and-pop business simply cannot compete with a large, well established franchisor in this area.

CHALLENGES TO FRANCHISING

It would be wrong to assume that franchising is without its limitations – franchising is NOT fail-safe.

▶ *Failure to follow the system*

On one hand, this may seem simplistic. "Of course I'd follow the system," you may say. "Why else would I shell out good money? The system is what I'm paying for."

But despite many cautions, the number one reason given for franchisees who fail is they did not follow the system. So why would a person fail to follow the system? There may be any number of reasons. For example, the franchisee did not focus 100% of their effort on the business because "the children needed braces so I had to pull back on my marketing," or even, "I think I have a better way of operating this business." We are all human and we need the flexibility to change as challenges present themselves. If you try to change the system and you end up with poor results, you must look in the mirror. The failure is not with the franchisor but with your choice not to use what you purchased – the rights to a proven system.

Incidentally, innovation does happen within franchise systems, and it is mostly driven by the franchisee community. After you have been in business for 18 months and have proven your ability to follow the system and create success, then work with your franchisor if you have an idea. If you both feel the idea has merit, test it in a controlled way in order to determine if it increases your business AND your profits.

▶ *Fees*

A franchisee must pay several fees to enter and remain within the system. There is a franchise fee that is paid one time up front. There is also a royalty that is typically paid on a weekly or monthly basis.

As a franchisee, you not only have to pay these fees, but you should consider it a part of your duty as a franchisee. The royalty stream is the franchisor's income and it is what allows the franchisor to re-invest into the system for ongoing improvements that benefit everybody. You want your franchisor to be powerful and successful. Without the dependable income stream known as royalties, the franchise system growth would be stifled, and so would the growth potential of individual franchisees.

You must be comfortable paying these fees and consider it your duty to the system to do so.

▶ *False Expectations*

One of the biggest problems new franchisees have when they enter a franchise system is false expectations. False expectations occur in two ways. First, some people think owning a franchise business is easy. Others fall in love with a franchise system without being fully informed.

In the first case, owning a franchise is not easy. A good franchise system does not reduce the work load, it simply allows you to focus your effort on more productive tasks while making fewer errors. You move through the learning curve faster. It may be more work than you have ever done before (and you may enjoy it more than working for someone else), but it is not easy.

The second point is that an emotionally based decision without facts to back it up almost always leads to false expectations. You look on an Internet site and find the perfect franchise. Immediately you are excited and are looking for positive reinforcement. Then you call the franchisor sales representative and they confirm your image and get you even more excited. Now you have a vision of how great the business will be and you choose to move forward. Guess what? Even if the franchise has a rock solid system with all the support and training you would ever need, you will still be disappointed because the reality will never live up to your imagination. This is a case of false expectations.

Regardless of what your initial gut level reaction is to a business opportunity, do your due diligence. It is a critical part of your learning process and is required to be sure you really know what it takes to be successful.

SUMMARY

Keep in mind *the good of the whole will trump the good of one* in the franchise world, and that philosophy is what helps to perpetuate the franchise. There's strength in the community of franchisees who all care about each other's well being. Franchisors will do what they need to do to protect the system as a whole.

And that *community* aspect may be the strongest differentiator between franchising and large corporations. Life in large corporations is often marked by political infighting, competitive behavior among departments and a tendency toward individual accolades and incentives.

In franchising, both franchisors and franchisees do all they can to strengthen the collective. And that ever growing pool of knowledge and trust – also known as *the system* – is what you become a part of in franchising.

"None of us is as smart as all of us."
– Japanese proverb on the power of a network

Chapter 7

Foundational Knowledge - The Franchise Disclosure Document

It isn't what the book costs;
it's what it will cost if you don't read it.
– Jim Rohn

The first glimpse of a Franchise Disclosure Document may be a bit daunting. After all, it is typically a thick, bound document with a lot of print and complexity.

But looks can be deceiving! The Franchise Disclosure Document is not only one of the most important consumer protections in American business, but it is also constructed and written in a way the average person can understand.

The earliest days of franchising were marked by some "bad actors" in the business, people who attracted the interest of the Federal Trade Commission (FTC). Because early franchisees were being victimized by false claims and unfulfilled promises, the FTC stepped in and created a series of laws revolving around franchising. In 1978, the FTC issued guidelines requiring that every franchisor publish, and share with prospective franchisees, a Franchise Disclosure Document. The Franchise Disclosure Document is primarily designed to protect franchisees.

Given today's growing franchising business environment, it is clear that Franchise Disclosure Document protection is actually helpful not only to franchisees, but also to franchisors who want their prospects to feel assured that high ethics are being observed. In short, it helps the entire franchising community.

The purpose of the Franchise Disclosure Document is to provide the franchisee with three things:

- **Transparency:** Prior to making any commitment, the prospective franchisee benefits from a significant amount of information that aids in the study of a franchise business.

- **Education:** The U.S. government wants the prospective franchisee to be well educated about the franchised business opportunity prior to committing time or resources.

- **Simplification:** Franchise Disclosure Documents are all structured fundamentally the same and are written in layman's language. Once you understand the format, you'll be able to easily review any franchise business.

DELIVERY AND ACCEPTANCE OF THE FRANCHISE DISCLOSURE DOCUMENT

Typically a copy is delivered by the franchisor, either electronically or by mail. The current trend is toward electronic disclosure and I expect, as time goes by, more and more franchisors will move to electronic delivery as a cost saving measure and for the convenience of prospects.

The Franchise Disclosure Document must be shared with the prospective franchisee at least 14 days prior to executing a franchise agreement. The FTC rule also requires the franchisor share the Franchise Disclosure Document when a prospect "reasonably requests" to see the document. Each franchisor will have their own policy in regard to when the Franchise Disclosure Document is shared with a prospective franchisee and what "reasonably" really means, but in all cases it must follow the basic rules outlined above.

Once you receive the Franchise Disclosure Document, you will be required to sign and return an Acknowledgement of Receipt. This receipt simply records the fact you received the document and records the date in which you were "disclosed."

As I mentioned above, once you receive a Franchise Disclosure Document, there is a mandatory waiting period of two weeks before any contract can be signed. This waiting period is designed to give you time to formulate questions and to make sure there is not a rush to conclude a deal without complete information being exchanged.

LOOKING FOR "RED FLAGS"

Sometimes people think accumulating lots of Franchise Disclosure Documents equates to having more knowledge about franchises, enough knowledge to make a judgment among franchise businesses. That's simply not the case.

The Franchise Disclosure Document does *not* tell you how the franchise competes against its competitors, who the competitors are and other qualitative aspects of the business. Instead, the Franchise Disclosure Document exclusively focuses on the factual information about the franchisor and the proposed relationship between the franchisor and franchisee.

Perhaps most important, the Franchise Disclosure Document reveals any red flags you should be aware of before making a judgment on the attractiveness of a franchise. The document helps you see past the flashy marketing and sales and allows you to refocus on an analytical view of the franchisor and the related opportunity.

THE FRANCHISE DISCLOSURE DOCUMENT CHECKLIST

What follows is a capsule summary of the items found in every Franchise Disclosure Document, regardless of the type of industry. With each item I will review:

- **Content:** An abbreviated summary of the factual contents found within Items 1 – 23, as defined in the FTC's Guideline document.

- **Purpose:** Discussion of why this passage exists and why the information is important to you.

- **Tips & Advice:** General information on how to interpret the information, or what the information means to you in practical terms and/or why it is significant.

Please keep in mind this information is directional in nature. Each franchisor will be unique; therefore you will have to use your own judgment as you interpret the specific information found in a given franchisor's disclosure document.

▶ Item 1: The Franchisor, Its Parents, Predecessors and Affiliates

Content: This section will include name, business address, business form, type of business, years in business, years in franchising and other businesses the franchisor, parent or affiliates may be involved in.

Purpose: In this passage, you find out how the business was started and what transfers of ownership have taken place. It also tells you the history of the franchise organization, parent corporations and discloses any other businesses in which the franchisor may be involved.

Tips & Advice: This section is designed to provide the foundational information you will need in order to fully understand the balance of the document. Pay special attention to predecessors, affiliated and parent companies. You want to leave this section knowing what business the franchisor is in, what kind of experience the organization has in the business and especially the history and ownership of the franchisor.

▶ Item 2: Business Experience

Content: A listing of all the key individuals, ranging from partners and directors to top executives with management responsibilities for the franchise. It will state the occupation and employer for each person over the past five years.

Purpose: This section is sort of a "group resume" as you qualify franchise prospects. A review of this section will give you an idea of the length and types of business experiences of your prospective business partners.

Tips & Advice: A franchise relationship generally extends over many years. Given the duration and the significance of the business relationship, you absolutely must know as much as you can about the people who will be your partners. As you examine the credentials of the franchise leadership team, give thought to what types of businesses they've been in and whether those experiences are meaningful for the business you're studying. Ask yourself, "If I have a problem with my business, do I think these folks have the knowledge and track record to assist me?" You also want to look for people that have significant experience in building franchise systems. Over the years I have noticed that if the top personnel have business, management and franchise experience, it generally results in stronger, healthier franchise systems, regardless of the current size of the franchisor.

▶ Item 3: Litigation

Content: A list of all the litigation the company is either currently involved in or anything the company has been convicted of over the last 10 years. It lists the details of the court cases so you can do your own research into them.

Purpose: A protection assuring the prospective franchisee is fully aware of past actions and actions pending.

Tips & Advice: You want to be careful if the franchisor has a large amount of activity in this area. Keep in mind the existence of litigation is not necessarily bad, such as litigation that enforces the integrity of the franchise system or if an action is labeled "ordinary routine litigation." The litigation to worry about is action that threatens the viability of the overall system, such as a patent claim that could harm or remove a key component in the product mix or a judgment that has long-term financial implications. You also want to be wary of systems that simply resort to legal action every time a franchisor or franchisee is unhappy. Every system will have disagreements from time to time. A healthy system is able to resolve the disagreement without resorting to legal action in the majority of cases.

▶ Item 4: Bankruptcy

Content: Shows whether any of the key officers have had any connection with bankruptcy proceedings over the past ten years.

Purpose: As with litigation, this item discloses information to the prospective franchisee about the financial history of the franchise's leadership team.

Tips & Advice: Obviously a single item of someone who may have been involved in a divorce is not a significant problem. In a large franchise, it is not unusual to discover that someone in management has been involved in some sort of bankruptcy proceedings. On the other hand, if the company chairman or, worse yet, the CFO, has been in bankruptcy proceedings recently, that obviously would not boost your confidence in the franchise.

▶ Item 5: Franchise Fees

Content: Simply the disclosure of all fees that must be paid to the franchisor prior to opening the business, the timing of the payment and whether there is any refundable aspect of the fees.

Purpose: While simple, the item should not be overlooked, as it clearly spells out what the franchisee must pay the franchisor.

Tips & Advice: Generally there are two types of fees that are normally paid prior to opening. The first is a franchise/territory/training fee. Some franchisors wrap this into one fee; others separate the payment for tax and reporting purposes. The other type of payment is product, material or equipment that must be purchased from the franchisor. If the franchisor is in the business of selling you material or equipment, you will be made aware of this fact here in Item 5.

▶ Item 6: Other Fees

Content: A disclosure of "other recurring or isolated fees or payments" that the franchisee must pay to the franchisor or its affiliates.

Purpose: This is disclosure of all other "ongoing fees" such as royalty and advertising. It is also a complete listing of any other potential "fine print" provisions. Any other fee that you could ever have to pay to the franchisor is listed here.

Tips & Advice: This is a great example of the transparency of the Franchise Disclosure Document and how it benefits the potential franchisee. Each fee listed will have explanatory notes, so be sure to read them. It's a good idea to give this section close examination because if there are any opportunities for "unexpected costs" to surface, they may be found here.

▶ Item 7: Estimated Initial Investment

Content: This item includes a comprehensive list of all the expenses you can reasonably expect to incur as you open the business.

Purpose: The objective of this section is to give you a reasonable expectation regarding the total cost to you should anticipate incurring as you open the business and operate the business for at least the first three months.

Tips & Advice: Like Item 6, this item is a tremendous safeguard for the franchisee. It includes all expenses right down to training fees, and travel and lodging associated with training. In addition, this item typically includes a minimum recommendation of set-aside cash flow as you start up the business and incidental, business related costs. Many franchises will specify a minimum of three months of living expenses, and quite often more. During the validation stage of your franchise investigation, this is an area in which you will want to ask the existing franchisees to disclose more detail. You'll find great detail on how to structure your financial conversation with the franchisees in Chapter 11.

▶ Item 8: Restrictions on Sources of Products and Services

Content: Item 8 tells you three things about procurement of products and services:

1) Which products or services are the franchisee required to purchase from the franchisor.

2) Which products or services are the franchisee required to purchase from approved, third party suppliers.

3) Which products or services are the franchisee free to purchase wherever they like.

Purpose: From the franchisor perspective, this item protects the integrity of the system's proprietary information and property. From the franchisee standpoint, it provides an awareness of both the obligations and opportunities for procuring the necessary materials to operate the business.

Tips & Advice: This section is important whenever there are a significant number of materials used in the delivery of the product or service and where the material costs are a significant percent of your P&L. There are normally three ways in which you will be allowed to purchase materials:

1) When a franchise company requires that you buy certain items

from them or exclusively from a single supplier, these purchased are considered **restricted**. For example, a food chain may have a specific recipe that distinguishes it from competitors, or a cleaning service may have equipment or supplies that are proprietary in nature. In other cases, the franchisor simply demands you purchase from them as an additional profit center. If you find a franchisor that has low or no royalties, it is guaranteed you will be required to purchase materials from them. This is their royalty.

2) The franchisor may designate **approved suppliers** for the franchisee to use. Vehicles and signage are examples of items the franchisor may acquire through certain contractors. In this case, you normally pay the approved supplier directly for the products you purchase.

3) **Unrestricted** purchases are the designation for routine items the franchisee may acquire without approval, such as towels, copier paper, etc.

▶ *Item 9: Franchisee's Obligations*

<u>Content:</u> A disclosure of all the "principal obligations of the franchisee under the franchise and other agreements" after the franchise agreement has been signed.

<u>Purpose:</u> To ensure the franchisee is aware of the nature and extent of all principal obligations they are assuming by becoming a franchisee.

<u>Tips & Advice:</u> This is a detailed section displayed in a table, and is another great example of the transparency of the disclosure document. It will refer to the sections in the franchise agreement the franchisee must be aware of. Read this section closely to allow you to more fully understand the franchisor's expectations and your obligations as a franchisee.

▶ *Item 10: Financing*

<u>Content:</u> A description of any financing terms the franchisor may make available to the franchisee, if any.

Purpose: This section is to inform the prospective franchisee about funding options available from the franchisor.

Tips & Advice: This is a brief passage in most franchise disclosure documents, as most franchisors do not offer in-house financing. Typically this item will state that. If there are financing terms, they will be listed in detail. Also, keep in mind that most franchisors have relationships with lenders who they commonly deal with. You should ask the franchisor representative what alternatives are available through third party lending sources.

▶ *Item 11: Franchisor's Assistance, Advertising, Computer Systems and Training*

Content: This is a list of the systems the franchisor brings to the table to assist the franchisee in becoming successful.

Purpose: This item is intended to provide the franchise prospect with a clear understanding of how the business relationship with the franchisor is structured.

Tips & Advice: It is critical to read this section very carefully. While the Content and Purpose are simply stated, the section itself is anything but simple. When you buy a franchise, you are purchasing the right to use the franchisor's operating system. This section provides details regarding that system—assistance that will be provided before, during and after opening. Here again is where transparency benefits the prospective franchisee as well as the franchisor, because only the obligations stated here can be expected by the franchisee. This is not to suggest that many franchisors do not go above and beyond in any respect. The point is that they are NOT obligated to do so. So once again, it is vital that you have an awareness of the franchisor's system and not make assumptions beyond the system as it is explicitly outlined.

▶ *Item 12: Territory*

Content: By definition, "...the minimum area granted to the franchisee. The franchisor may use an area encompassed within a specific radius, a distance sufficient to encompass a specified population or another specific designation."

Purpose: The franchisee, where appropriate, needs to know what restrictions are in place to give them the best possible chance of success.

Tips & Advice: This topic is especially critical in business categories where population density drives the business model. For example, if you invest in a restaurant franchise, you want reasonable assurance you and a fellow franchisee are not competing for the same client base. It is important that you fully understand this because it is a continual source of disagreement in large, mature systems. "Impact Issues," or "encroachment," as they are often called, occur when a franchisee thinks the franchisor opened another location too close in proximity and that they have been negatively impacted as a result. Make sure you understand what protection you are purchasing. On the other hand, keep in mind some very successful systems have no exclusive territories at all. You'll find more about this in Chapter 8.

Often, new franchisees want as much territory as possible. Sometimes a franchise company will discount the fees of additional territories if they are purchased at the same time. Also, some franchisors may use the last official census data to determine the population base in a territory. While you always want the most current data, if the franchisor is using older data and your area has grown rapidly since the census was taken, the additional population can be considered a bonus for you!

▶ *Item 13: Trademarks*

Content: All registered trademarks of the franchisor are specified here, including all the registration information for those trademarks.

Purpose: Franchisees are advised about the "trade dress," including the logos, symbols, trade names, etc. available for their use. More importantly, the registration information confirms the franchisee has critical protection in two important areas:

1) Exclusivity from competitors using the same trademarks.

2) Assurance the trademarks will be available for the long term.

Tips & Advice: This item is brief, but important. Virtually all franchisors will clearly outline the complete and proper registration of their logos and trade names. This is one of the first things a franchisor does when setting up their system to franchise. Do be careful to look for areas in which the trademark may be contested. If the franchisor does not have the name or logo properly registered, this is a reason to "just say no" to the opportunity.

▶ *Item 14: Patents, Copyrights and Proprietary Information*

<u>Content:</u> If the franchisor owns rights to patents, copyrights or proprietary information that are material to the franchise, the franchisor will describe these and their relationship to the franchisee in this section.

<u>Purpose:</u> Again, just as with Item 13, this section will give you an idea of whether the franchisor is well protected.

<u>Tips & Advice:</u> The same red flag warning is given here as in Item 13. Just imagine for a moment how important the Colonel's secret recipe has been to KFC® over the years and what the consequences would have been if that recipe had not been protected from usage by competitors.

▶ *Item 15: Obligation to Participate in the Actual Operation of the Franchise*

<u>Content:</u> This describes how much direct involvement the franchisee is required to have in the actual operation of the business.

<u>Purpose:</u> By stating the terms explicitly, the franchisor may be preventing a future conflict with a franchisee over an issue of performance. If a franchise unit was found to be underperforming, one of the first things to be examined would be the question of the franchisee's effort.

<u>Tips & Advice:</u> It may sound unusual to specify how much day-to-day participation is required to be successful, but because people may have various business interests, they need to know if the franchise company allows passive ownership. This declaration serves the dual purpose of giving the franchisee a realistic expectation while at the same time protecting the franchisor against a claim by a franchisee who was not fully engaged.

▶ *Item 16: Restrictions on What the Franchisee May Sell*

<u>Content:</u> This is a description of the "conditions imposed by the franchisor on the goods or services that the franchisee may sell."

Purpose: This protects the standards and uniformity of the franchise system.

Tips & Advice: If you are going to buy a business that has a specific type of product, it is likely that the restrictions to that product will be delineated clearly in this section. To use a fairly obvious example, such a restriction assures a McDonald's franchisee will open the store each day with an expectation of selling Big Macs, not cell phones.

▶ Item 17: Renewal, Termination, Transfer and Dispute Resolution

Content: This section "summarizes the provisions of the franchise and other agreements dealing with termination, renewal, transfer, dispute resolution and other important aspects of the franchise relationship."

Purpose: To provide both parties with clearly specified remedies for any disputes that may arise.

Tips & Advice: In this section, the franchisee is directed to the specific places in the franchise agreement that relates to renewal, termination, transfer and dispute resolution. You will find a table that tells exactly how any of these matters are to be resolved. What's really helpful about this item is the breakdown in layman's terms of all possible outcomes, including worst-case scenarios.

▶ Item 18: Arrangements with Public Figures

Content: This notes relationships with public figures.

Purpose: The franchisee is advised about the business relationship the franchise has with a public figure and prevents confusion about how the franchisee may use the name and other images of the public figure.

Tips & Advice: George Foreman's contract with Meineke Car Care Center®, for example, is listed in the franchise disclosure document. But the existence of a promotional tie-in with Foreman does not mean the Meineke franchisee has carte blanche privileges to use the former boxing champ's image in advertisements. It also does not guarantee George Foreman and Meineke will sign to extend the relationship.

▶ *Item 19: Financial Performance Representations*

<u>Content:</u> This is "information given to a prospective franchisee by, on behalf of or at the direction of the franchisor or its agent, from which a specific level or range of actual or potential sales, costs, income or profit from franchised or non-franchised units may be easily ascertained."

<u>Purpose:</u> In short, the declaration of a Financial Performance Representation gives the prospect an expectation of how much money can be made from the business. On the other hand, if no representation is made, information must be collected through interviewing the existing franchisees.

<u>Tips & Advice:</u> In early franchise history, this is the area that triggered a lot of the involvement of the FTC. Less than reputable franchisors made unfounded claims about the income people could earn through their franchises. Obviously, anyone looking at a business wants to know how they make money, but misleading people is unacceptable. This is why Item 19 is important. Any representation a franchisor makes must be in writing and must be in the Franchise Disclosure Document. Today, the majority of franchisors do not make financial performance representations for a couple of reasons. For one thing, the franchisor may not have complete, accurate profit and loss information on the franchisee level. It can be time consuming and expensive to collect that data. Perhaps the stronger motivation for not making a representation is the history of litigation associated with these types of statements. Today, only about 25% of franchisors provide some type of limited performance representation.

If the franchisor chooses to make a Financial Performance Representation in Item 19, then the franchisor can discuss earnings with you up to the extent of the claim. In other words, if the franchisor provides gross sales averages, they can discuss gross sales averages – but not net profitability. If the franchisor does not make a financial performance representation, they are legally prohibited from discussing earnings with you.

Whether the franchisor makes a financial performance representation or not, the existing franchisees themselves are the best source of information. In Chapter 12, we will deal with the critical issue of how to develop a model profit and loss statement.

▶ *Item 20: Outlets and Franchisee Information*

<u>**Content:**</u> Several tables are detailed in this item and each table includes three years of data. Table one is a summary of system wide outlets. Table two is "transfers of outlets from franchisees to new owners" (other than the Franchisor). Table three provides information on the status of franchised outlets. Table four provides information on the status of company-owned outlets. Table five is a table of projected new franchised outlets.

<u>**Purpose:**</u> This information is provided primarily to give you a numerical breakdown of locations and growth or regression trends.

<u>**Tips & Advice:**</u> Many people look at this section on a micro level. They go to their state and ask, "Why was there a transfer in my state two years ago?" Although you may want to ask this type of question, I think the more relevant questions relate to overall system wide trends. Has the system grown over the past three years? Has more than 10 % of the system changed hands in any given year? Have there been an excessive number of abandonments? This is an important section—don't overlook the forest for the trees. In regard to the last table, projected new franchised outlets, you can, in most cases, ignore it. There are some franchisors that are highly focused on specific markets, and that may be relevant, but the fact is that most franchisors just don't have a good enough crystal ball to be able to predict this with any level of accuracy.

▶ *Item 21: Financial Statements*

<u>**Content:**</u> This section includes balance sheets covering the past two years and income statements for the past three years. These "financial statements (for the franchisor) must be in accordance with generally accepted accounting principles."

<u>**Purpose:**</u> The obvious purpose of this section is to give the franchise prospect a clear picture of the solvency of the franchisor.

<u>**Tips & Advice:**</u> Some people think these may be the financial statements of the individual franchisees, but they are not. These are simply the audited financial statements of the franchisor for the past two to three years. If you do not have a background in finance and/or you do

not clearly understand the statements, this is an area you may want a trusted advisor to examine.

▶ Item 22: Contracts

<u>Content:</u> The franchisor will attach a copy of all agreements proposed for use or in use in your state regarding the offering of a franchise, including the Franchise Agreement, sample leases, and Options and Purchase Agreements.

<u>Purpose:</u> This section itself is brief, but it contains references to the exhibits that constitute the legal relationship between you and the franchisor.

<u>Tips & Advice:</u> Your alertness is critical in this section, as it refers to the actual legal documents you will be signing should you choose to become a franchisee. While it is an invaluable guide, the Franchise Disclosure Document is not a legal document—but all the exhibits listed in Item 22 are. Most notable, of course, is the actual Franchise Agreement itself. Don't think the Franchise Agreement is the only legal contact for you to be concerned with. Every other exhibit, such as a Territory Addendum, is a separate, legally-binding contract to be executed by both franchisor and franchisee. So don't be fooled by the brevity of Item 22, and be sure to pay careful attention to each of the exhibits listed there.

▶ Item 23: Receipt

<u>Content:</u> This is simply a one-page document the prospective franchisee signs to acknowledge that the Franchise Disclosure Document was received.

<u>Purpose:</u> There is no obligation related to this signature page; it is merely an acknowledgement of receipt and a listing of your rights under the FTC.

<u>Tips & Advice:</u> There is no need for concern about signing this page and returning it to the franchisor.

▶ *Exhibits*

A number of exhibits are found after Items 1 - 23. These exhibits are important to your full understanding of the contractual relationship. Whether you choose to use a lawyer to review the exhibits or not, it is critical you review the information in these exhibits yourself and attempt to understand the information. I will touch on this topic more in Chapter 14. These exhibits change from franchise to franchise, but they generally include the following:

- A template version of the Franchise Agreement you would sign as a franchisee

- A template version of any other legal contract you may need to sign as a franchisee including guarantees, leases, service agreements, etc.

- A full list of all franchisees as of the date of the document including names, addresses and phone numbers

- Table of Contents from the Operational Manual

- Corporate financial statements

SUMMARY

As you study a franchise business, you will find the Franchise Disclosure Document to be an important reference tool. It both provides information raises questions that need to be researched further, so put your highlight marker and sticky tabs to good use with this valuable document.

However, when reviewing this document you should not expect to learn about *why* you should join a franchise. The Franchise Disclosure Document is not designed to share this type of information with you. The sole purpose is to ensure that you are an educated consumer and to make sure you have information on critical points prior to becoming a franchisee. Read the Franchise Disclosure Document carefully, ask the franchisor about anything you don't understand or are concerned about, ask the franchisees if they have any of the same concerns you have and then use your judgment to make a business decision about the information found within the Franchise Disclosure Document.

Please go to www.educatedfranchisee.com if you would like additional information on disclosure documents, how they are structured, or would like suggestions for additional reading.

Chapter 8

Foundational Knowledge - Alternatives In Franchising

You have brains in your head
You have feet in your shoes
You can steer yourself
Any direction you choose

— Theodor S. Geisel (Dr. Seuss)

Topics in this chapter are among the most widely discussed when referring to franchising, but all too often they are sources of misinformation, especially when it comes to examining the types of franchise opportunities available in the marketplace. Our objective here is to provide clarity about items that define the relationship between the franchisor and the new business owner:

- The various contractual franchisor/franchisee relationships

- Different types of territory protections

- Fees: franchise fees, royalties, marketing fees

- Comparing franchisors

- Comparing industries

You'll learn the details that are commonly "top of mind" for prospective franchisees.

The logical starting point in this area of investigation is to learn the different ways a franchise relationship may be structured.

TYPES OF FRANCHISE RELATIONSHIPS

A common misconception is that franchising is only for the small business owner. Some believe franchising is suitable for the person who wants to make sandwiches, but not for the person that wants to build a serious, substantial business empire. The fact is, depending on your goals, franchisees can build significant, multi-million dollar businesses. One example of a successful, high-yield endeavor is that of a former franchisee of Applebee's®, doing business as Apple South, who had 264 restaurants. In this section, we'll examine the various business structures that allow a person to scale their franchise to fit their personal objectives. We will begin by discussing what it means to be a Direct Franchisee, Area Developer, Master Franchisor and Sub-Franchisee.

Direct Franchise

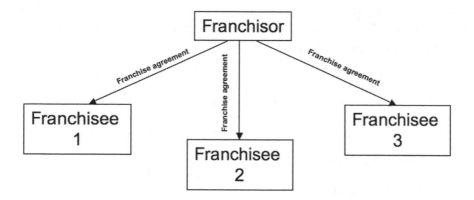

Direct franchising is the most common franchise relationship. It is a two-tiered relationship between a franchisor and a franchisee. More than 90% of franchise licenses are direct franchises. The franchisee is the person who operates the specific business. The franchisee agrees to assume operational responsibilities by signing a contract with the franchisor, whose obligation is to provide a system model, training and support.

In many ways direct franchising is the easiest to understand. The relationship is the simplest to structure, has the lowest investment and has the lowest risk, if for no other reason than the fact that fewer parties are involved.

Area Development

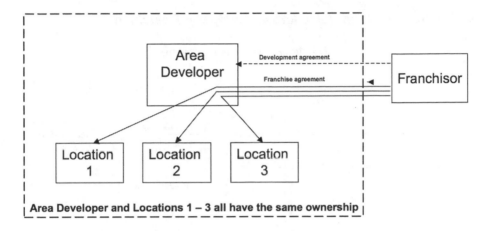

Area Developer and Locations 1 – 3 all have the same ownership

An Area Development agreement is also a two-tiered structure between a franchisor and a franchisee. But in this instance, the scale is significantly larger and more complex. It is for the business investor who has the financial backing and management ability to fund and build a larger organization.

Under an Area Development agreement, the franchisee buys the right to own and operate multiple locations. The franchisor sells an entire geographic territory in which the franchisee may build, own and operate multiple locations. A good example is Panera Bread®. According to their web site, "Panera does not sell single-unit franchises." Panera sells you the rights to a development area and would typically require you build, own and operate a minimum of 15 stores over a six-year period. You must have a net worth of at least $7.5 million and liquidity of $3 million in order to build this type of program. Not all area development programs require this large an investment, but the investment is always larger than a single unit, direct franchise relationship.

And though the Area Development agreement is a two-party agreement, it is more complex than the direct franchise model because two contracts are required—the Development Agreement and then Franchise Agreements that link each location back to the franchisor.

If you are attracted to the larger opportunity an Area Development contract affords, be ready and able to comply with the build-out terms and conditions of the franchisor. If you do not build out the territory in the prescribed time period, the franchisor usually reserves the right to remove your development rights for future stores.

▶ *Master Franchisor (also known as Master Franchise)*

Master Franchise Agreement

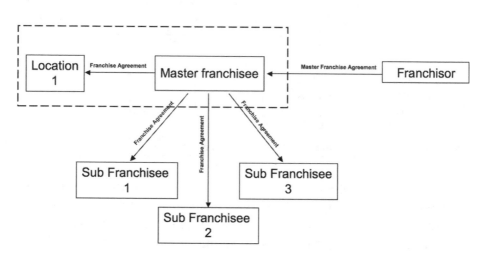

Another type of franchise relationship that has evolved in recent years is a more complex, three-tiered structure called the Master Franchisor model. Under this model, the franchisor sells the franchise sales rights to a franchisee, often referred to as a master franchisor, for a geographic territory. The master franchisor in turn assumes the responsibility for selling franchises.

Both the opportunities and the responsibilities are much larger for the master franchisor in this model. The investment level is typically much higher than an investment at the direct franchise level. Plus, the master franchisor shares in the responsibility to support the sub-franchisees within the master franchisor territory.

Along with the added responsibility comes significant opportunity for the master franchisor, such as shares of franchise sales and royalty payments, which will be discussed later in this chapter. In addition, the master franchisor commonly enjoys a collaborative relationship with the franchisor in overall marketing, system development and sub-franchisee support.

In a master franchising relationship, the master franchisor often has the opportunity, if not obligation, to own and operate a franchise unit. That sort of experience gives the master franchisor additional credibility with the prospective sub-franchisee and an added revenue opportunity. It also can work as a local showcase and training center for the concept.

▶ Sub-Franchisee

A sub-franchisee is simply a franchisee who executes a franchise agreement with the master franchisor. It can be a tremendous bonus for a sub-franchisee to sign on with a master franchisor that provides great support and has a strong track record. At the same time, it can be a problem for the sub-franchisee if the master franchisor is not strong; therefore, it makes good sense to research the strength and ability of both the franchisor and master franchisor.

TYPES OF TERRITORIAL PROTECTION

Most people think of *exclusive territories* when they think of franchising. Most franchisors provide some sort of exclusivity or territory definition, particularly in retail segments where the business depends on a certain population base.

That protection can be defined in a number of ways. The territory can be broken down by city, by county, by a series of zip codes, or even a radius of a certain number of miles. Regardless of what method is used to define the territory, it is important for the franchise agreement to spell out the definitions explicitly.

There are various types of exclusive territorial protection. Some franchise systems provide absolute protection, while others may prevent you from marketing in another owner's territory, with no prohibition against you making actual sales to customers residing in another territory.

In location-driven businesses, you typically find a radius formula in place, with no other franchisee permitted to establish a location or market within that radius. Often, beyond the franchisee's radius, is a larger area subject to "impact study." The impact study comes into play if somebody is considering opening another location close to your defined territory. The impact study would show whether it would be viable for another franchisee to be located nearby. Many food franchises use this approach.

Keep in mind, however, that an exclusivity protection only protects the franchisee from others within the same franchise company. It does nothing to prevent competitors from opening a location right across the street. This limitation is evident when you see a large group of fast-food chains as neighbors in a commercial district, a common occurrence.

Semi-exclusive territory protection is offered by some franchisors, with some interesting advantages. In this approach, the franchisee does not enjoy exclusivity within a particular geographic area. The franchisor may measure a particular county, for example, and arrive at a business judgment regarding the business opportunity available for franchisees in that area. Then the franchisor would place a restriction on the number of franchises it would sell in that area.

The Chem-Dry® franchise, which is the largest carpet cleaning franchise in the country and a division of Home Depot®, serves as a great model of semi-exclusive territory protection. They take a geographic territory and measure the total amount of opportunity within that area. Chem-Dry then divides the territory according to the number of franchisees who could be successful, not directing the specific locations from which they would operate. They may calculate that three franchisees could maximize the investment in a certain area and then leave it up to the individual franchisees to determine their locations.

HomeVestors®, the "We Buy Ugly Houses" company, has a similar approach. They maximize their system by allowing a limited number of franchisees to work together in a marketplace to secure the best billboard advertising. The leads are then shared on a rotating basis, giving the franchisees an equal opportunity for growth.

The advantage of semi-exclusivity is the leverage that franchisees can apply as they share marketing expenses and collaborate in other marketing methods, as well as operational practices. In a semi-exclusive territory, neighboring franchisees may serve as backup sources of labor in the event an employee at a particular location does not show up for work.

Client exclusivity is employed by franchise systems that are mostly relationship driven. In this type of franchise, the franchisee has complete geographic freedom, with exclusivity assigned to a particular client or client group as the business relationship is established with that particular customer. To someone considering new business entry, a lack of geographic protection may seem like a serious potential pitfall, but for some types of businesses, geographic divisions would actually serve to limit, not enhance, the business.

Relationship-driven, referral-based businesses, for example, would be negatively impacted by boundaries that prohibit the owners from taking advantage of the built-in networking circles they may bring with them. Professional services firms, which operate under models similar to law firms and CPA firms, can thrive even when competitors have office space in the same building. The growth of such businesses depends greatly on the referrals that existing customers provide, and a geographic restriction could stifle that sort of activity.

FEES

▶ Franchise fees

The franchise fee is the upfront fee charged when you purchase a business. It is the amount of money you pay in order to secure the rights for a specific period of time, as outlined in the Franchise Agreement. Think of it in the context of an initiation fee you would pay to join a private club.

In this case, the franchisor is giving you either a geographic territory or access to a particular group of clients or customers. In other words, you're receiving the right to use an asset that belongs to the franchisor—both the right to the system and the right to the opportunity/ territory. Also, franchise fees are used to offset the startup costs incurred by the franchisor for initial training and support programs. For most franchisors, the franchise fee is not an income source. Instead, the franchise fee is generally an offset of the costs of maintaining an infrastructure that helps the franchisees get up and running.

Franchise fees can range from $5,000 to well over $100,000 for a significant opportunity. The average is around $25,000 to $30,000. Some franchisors will break up the franchise fee and label separate charges as "training fees" or "territory fees," but those distinctions are generally for tax purposes. Regardless of labels, you can look at all those fees in the collective as the franchise fee.

▶ *Royalties*

Royalties are weekly or monthly payments incurred for the life of the Franchise Agreement. It's important to understand the purpose of royalties. The royalty allows the franchisor to exist. It allows the franchisor to build and maintain a comprehensive support system, to aggressively develop its marketing programs and it allows the franchisor to innovate and stay on the cutting edge of their industry.

Without the royalty stream, there would be no franchise system. And remember, the proven system is the most valuable aspect of what the franchisee is buying.

Percent-based royalty is the most common form of royalty in franchising. The percent-based royalties range widely, anywhere from 1% to 30% of gross sales, with an average of about 7.5%. In some systems, this percentage rate is reduced with increased franchisee sales volume.

This format is advantageous to a franchisee in the earlier phases of the business, especially in the first year when the business starts building its customer base from scratch. As the business matures however, the royalty payments will continue to grow in proportion as sales volume grows.

Sales volume is where the franchisor and franchisee enjoy a common bond—an advantage of percent-based royalties. In a percent-based structure, both franchisor and franchisee are motivated toward the same objective, raising sales volume, which in turn tends to drive the bottom line.

Fixed royalties are less common, but they represent a different school of thought about how to motivate franchisees. Under a fixed royalty scenario, a franchisee pays the same amount each month regardless of sales volume. The royalty may seem onerous at the outset, but the royalty can become very attractive as the business grows. In other words, you get to keep more of what you earn as you grow into a successful business owner.

Also, fixed royalties are clear-cut and have less room for interpretation, or misinterpretation, as franchisees make their royalty payments. In a fixed royalty system, there are rarely disagreements about the calculation of royalty payments.

Some systems do not demand a royalty. Some people consider this to be a strong positive—I would tell you to be careful. The franchisor must make money to survive, and without a royalty, the franchisor must make money through the sale of products and supplies to the franchisees. Generally, the franchisors who make their money from selling products and supplies may not disclose the amount of profit they are making.

▶ *An observation about royalty levels*

Sometimes a potential franchisee will do research about franchise companies in the same category, let's say cleaning services, and will find their eyes trained on the direct comparison among royalty payments. If they see low, medium and high royalty payments for three different companies, they may be inclined to think the one with the lowest royalty payment is the best choice.

Without more complete information, those figures can be misleading. Royalty payments will figure into the business as a line item expense, nothing more. The important factor to focus on is the profit—what you take home at the end of the day. The questions you need to ask yourself are these: What is the difference? What am I getting from one company that I'm not getting from another?

You will find that many successful, high quality franchisors have a higher royalty than their less successful competitors. The higher royalty is frequently reinvested back into the business and the system becomes stronger as a result. These companies often have superior service to both end-user customers as well as franchisees. In some cases a higher royalty may be well worth it.

▶ *Advertising contribution/commitment*

Advertising is another franchisee expense, and works in two ways in a franchise system.

1) **Advertising contribution:** This is a certain amount of money the franchisee gives to the franchisor on a regular basis; it's not income to the franchisor. This money goes into a fund for projects that help the franchisor and franchisees market, such as brochures, posters, photography, print materials, billboards, TV advertisements, national print advertising, web site design, search engine optimization and even national trade shows to promote the brand name and reputation. All franchisees contribute to the advertising fund and have the right to use materials created with the use of the advertising fund money. The advertising fund is a "transparent fund." Each franchisee has the right to review a full accounting of all contributions and expenses to ensure the money is being spent to promote the brand.

2) **Advertising commitment:** This is an amount of money required to be spent in the local market by the franchisee to drive business. This is the same money that every successful business owner should be spending to promote their business. The only difference is, in a franchise system, the amount is quantified and agreed upon ahead of time.

It would be wrong to view marketing obligations as onerous requirements imposed by the franchisor. Failing to market may be the biggest mistake any business owner can make, so it's really a plus when the franchisor provides guidance in this area. Under marketing, not under capitalization, is the biggest barrier to a franchisee's success, particularly in the early stages of the business.

COMPARING FRANCHISORS

Just as fees must be judged in a larger context, the size and age of franchise systems must also be considered carefully.

Of course, large franchise systems have some distinct advantages, some of which are obvious. They have more franchisees, their systems are more proven, they have a longer track record. For the most part, they have fewer "hiccups" in the business startup phase.

One disadvantage may be smaller territories and higher franchise fees, meaning you will basically be getting less territory but more system for the dollar than you would pay for a younger system. In essence, you're paying a surcharge for a more proven system and lower risk.

A younger system may charge lower franchise fees and offer larger territories. The absence of a track record and franchisees to validate the system means the risk may be greater for the franchisee. The lower fees and larger territory allow the risk/reward equation to remain in balance.

Although there may be more bumps in the road with a smaller, newer system, the rewards can be substantial for those who invest their money and faith in the system and get in on the ground floor. This type of system is a better fit for a more entrepreneurial individual.

For example, as Budget Blinds® embarked on their early franchising, an entrepreneur who strongly believed in the concept bought the exclusive rights to the majority of the Tampa Bay metropolitan area in Florida.

Fast forward 15 years and Budget Blinds® is now the largest franchise system in the country for installing window treatments. They have added more than 900 franchisees and are sold out in a number of markets.

Because the franchisee was willing to join the system in its early days, they were granted a territory that is substantially larger than current Budget Blinds® territories. The franchisee controls an asset that has grown substantially in value should they wish to sell their business in the future. In essence, it's like a real estate play.

COMPARING INDUSTRIES

Finally, the same kind of analysis should be applied to industries within franchising. Many people think franchisors are responsible for creating new industries, but, interestingly, franchisors are more inclined to enhance and develop large proven industries.

New industries are generally developed by bootstrap entrepreneurs who venture boldly into the marketplace with "something to prove." The failure rate in those cases is very high, but from the successes come the opportunities that franchisors exploit. Franchisors are very good at creating better systems for competing within existing industries.

New industries are high risk, primarily because the marketplace has to be educated about what the problem or need is in the first place, and then why the solution is so valuable. Naturally, the rewards are high when a new idea catches on, but the entrepreneur must first educate consumers on the need and then sell the solution.

Most franchisors thrive in proven industries in which they have identified unlimited demand and/or a critical shortage of professionals who are providing quality solutions.

The new systems that are brought into an industry have the advantage of perfecting a model and, with economies of scale, leveraging their systemization to sizable advantage over the mom and pops already operating within the category.

SUMMARY

Overall, franchising is more varied than most people think. There is something for everyone in terms of structures, types of businesses and price levels. As the prospective franchisee explores the wide variety of options, it is important to make comparisons that go deeper than the price tags.

For example, don't be fooled by a comparison of, say, three franchises in which one of the franchises emphasizes low royalties, seemingly a very favorable factor. Keep the old maxim "you get what you pay for" in mind in such situations. Look more deeply into the question of what you're getting for your royalty payment, not just the amount of the royalty payment.

Get past the surface level and probe the more meaningful aspects of making a significant financial and emotional investment.

Chapter 9

Targeting Franchisors To Investigate

The odds of hitting your TARGET go
up dramatically when you aim at it.
— Mal Pancoast

At first glance, targeting franchisors may seem to be an easy task. After all, isn't it just a matter of finding some names and starting to call them? In reality, this is an underrated aspect of franchise investigation in terms of both the time it takes and the process of selection.

Over the course of an investigation, you are likely to spend 30 hours or more in order to fully understand a franchise system. For people managing multiple priorities, your investigation should take a month, assuming a commitment of one hour per day. It's a lot of hard work, because you want to be careful in your selection. You don't want to waste your valuable time investigating companies that are not good matches for you.

Fundamentally, there are two paths you can follow in your franchise investigation: You can explore on your own, using all the resources that are available to you, or you can seek out the help of a third party, a franchise consultant, to guide you.

Both have their advantages and disadvantages, but the goal is the same—to narrow down the field of prospects to two or three good possibilities to investigate in depth and then to conduct a thorough review of those finalists.

EXPLORING INDEPENDENTLY

The first step in conducting your investigation of franchisors is to turn, once again, to your vision, reviewing the goals and objectives we discussed earlier. With the large number of franchise opportunities in the marketplace, you could lose a lot of valuable time without having a clear idea of your direction. You must know what you are looking for in order to be able to recognize it.

With your vision clearly in mind and an analysis of your skills completed, it's time to examine the many sources of information available to you.

▶ *Websites*

Today websites are probably the primary source of information gathering that people use. Just type the word "franchise" in any of the popular search engines, such as Google or Yahoo, and you'll find an extensive list of franchise information sources. Like many things on the web, the quantity generally exceeds the quality of sites, as some sites are far more valuable than others. To find a list of high quality, reputable franchise websites, you can visit www.educatedfranchisee.com.

When you explore any of the good quality sites, you'll find a lot of information—enough information to keep you busy literally for hours. The good websites will include tools that allow you to sort among concepts and levels of investment.

You also need to be careful in exploring websites. For one thing, nothing assures that the information you find there is accurate. These websites are driven by advertising, so the franchisors who advertise there are obviously going to control the content that is posted. As a result, you'll find information with a heavy marketing slant to it.

In addition, because "money talks" on the web, you will only see the companies that pay to advertise. As a result, you may not get a complete picture of the marketplace. Be cautious about rankings that are posted by the various sites, as the rankings are not predictors of future success. It's a little like the ranking of mutual funds, which are often based on what performance was like according to last year's data.

Websites are great places to start and provide a vast amount of quality information at the 30,000 foot level, but they will not be able to answer your questions about whether the franchise fits your vision, your skills and your goals. Only a quality due diligence effort will accomplish this.

▶ Trade shows

Trade shows can be a great opportunity to meet franchisors, or their agents, face-to-face. Typically the trade show atmosphere is conducive to short, cordial conversations, during which you can get answers to many of your questions. More importantly, you get the chance to develop a rapport with the people you may consider as business partners.

In many instances you may have the chance to actually see, or in the case of food franchises, taste, the product. You'll also have the opportunity to collect all the relevant brochures that a company has to offer, which saves you time during your investigation.

Unfortunately, trade shows are becoming smaller and less frequent than in the past. Franchisors now rely more on the Internet for distributing information to prospects. As a result, participation in trade shows may be limited to smaller franchisors whose offices are near the exposition site.

Another limitation of trade shows are the sales reps who are typically "working the booth". These sales reps are generally very nice people but remember that it is their job to give you a positive impression of the franchise opportunity. This means, of course, that trade shows are good places to gather information, but not good places to secure an unbiased view of the franchise.

▶ What's going on in your neighborhood?

Simplistic as it may sound, it may be useful to literally explore your own neighborhood to get a feel for what franchises are growing in popularity. As you take a drive around your area, you will notice franchise outlets ranging from fast food to automobile services to tax preparation.

If you're an assertive person, willing to follow up your curiosity, you can drop into the business to speak with the owner and to observe the work flow. In fact, spending some time among customers is probably the most revealing.

While the "drop in" approach may be good for getting the feel of how the business operates, it does not give you a good idea of whether the franchise is profitable—or whether it's a franchise at all—if the owner is not available, or willing, to talk with you.

► *Magazines and other media reports*

Frequently newspaper and magazine articles examine franchising and franchising opportunities. These can be great places to learn more about different ideas and approaches.

There are a number of reputable magazines that focus on franchising. You can find a list of these in the Resource section at www. educatedfranchisee.com. It would make sense to review these. At the same time, be on the lookout for articles in reputable non-franchising specific magazines and newspapers such as *Forbes, The Wall Street Journal* or *Newsweek*. Many times reliable sources are able to give you insight into future trends in a variety of industries and often present the information in an unbiased way.

On the other hand, always keep this in mind: A positive trend does not mean that you should jump into the business. It must match your vision, skills, investment and overall objectives.

WORKING WITH A FRANCHISE CONSULTANT

For the same reason that working with a buyer's agent makes sense when looking for the perfect home, working with a franchise consultant can provide tremendous leverage to the prospective franchise buyer. Yes, downsides are possible, but for the most part, franchise consulting is a high growth business because both franchisee prospects AND franchisors get such great value from the relationship.

A franchise consultant plays a role similar to that of a "headhunter" in the job recruitment process, playing the matchmaker who links two parties with the potential to work well together.

► *How franchise consulting began and how it works*

Not long ago in the United States, franchise consulting services were unavailable. All the investigation and research was done through magazines and follow-up phone calls.

As franchisors and future franchisees have grown in sophistication, it has become apparent that the use of a knowledgeable, experienced third party to make high quality matches saves both time and money. Why is this?

For franchisors, finding the perfect franchisee that will be highly successful in their system takes significant time and effort. Less than 1% of the people that directly contact a franchisor will become a franchisee; however, a franchisor has to staff up to deal with the 99% that are either not qualified, not serious or not a good fit.

At the same time, prospective franchisees often find that franchisors can be unresponsive. Even though the lack of responsiveness may be for a good reason, such as having sold out the area or simply a shortage of staff, this can be very frustrating to a potential franchisee. Determining which franchisor is interested in their area and in their skills can be challenging.

In many ways, franchise consulting has matured in the same way the home buyer has embraced the buyer's agent. Twenty years ago home buyers would see a sign, look at a house, go to the agent's office and look through the agent's book of listings to find out what was available in the market. Today's home buyer leverages time by using a buyer's agent to streamline the process by identifying properties that match the buyer's profile. Once identified, they look only at the houses in the right neighborhood, of the right size and the right price, thereby reserving more time to inspect the properties.

The same approach applies to identifying high quality franchise opportunities in your area, as the franchise consultant takes a lot of the duress out of the investigation process by interviewing the prospect and then presenting good matches for that person. As with a buyer's agent or an executive recruiter, the consultant's service is free to the buyer, so the prospective franchisee feels more comfortable in the relationship with the consultant.

Reaching a consultant is very easy, as you can find the companies listed on all the likely web searches. Typically when you contact a consulting company, you'll be assigned a consultant. The consultant walks you through a series of steps including completing a questionnaire and a consultation in order to build a model of the "perfect business" for the client.

The consultant then identifies target companies for you and presents a range of options, typically three businesses. The client always has the option of discarding any or all of the presented franchises, but quite often there will be at least one franchise among the first three that will make a good match for the prospect.

Finally, the consultant plays an advisory role as the prospect prepares for, and then actually conducts, the due diligence process, which involves talking in detail with franchisees.

▶ Pros and cons of using a franchise consultant

Time is money. Consider what a precious commodity time is today, and you can see why an experienced guide who saves you time and energy is highly valued. Seasoned franchise consultants will only work with pre-screened, solid franchise organizations. A trusted advisor will not waste time looking at franchisors that are sold out, don't really match your skills or vision or simply have a poor success record.

It's a service that is completely free of charge to the candidate. That's a big plus.

On the other hand, franchise consultants have their limitations as well. Even the industry leaders only represent franchises they have surveyed and present what they consider to be solid opportunities. So, if you're hoping to survey the entire field of thousands of franchisor companies, it probably won't happen with a franchise consultant.

Moreover, not all franchise consultants are created equal. The "luck of the draw" when a franchise company assigns consultants can result in an unfavorable match between the consultant and prospect. You will find a great franchise consultant will be:

- Experienced in business ownership and in franchising

- An active listener

- Someone with your best interests in mind at all times

- A person who you can trust

- And finally, someone who will be open and honest in their communication with you

The best franchise consultants know the traits, skills and personalities of top owners within each franchise system. They will take the time to get to know you, your vision, your goals, your skills and your personality. The most successful franchise consultants are the ones who carefully examine the alternatives for a client and try to find the best match.

SUMMARY

It all comes down to personal preferences and the variables that govern your specific situation. If you are the kind of person that likes to pull out a shotgun when you are aiming at something in hopes of connecting with the target, then it might be best to go it on your own using any number of the resources outlined in this chapter.

On the other hand, if time is important to you and you prefer to use a rifle when going after your target, then the help of a franchise consultant may be valuable allowing you to spend more time researching the best franchisors for you.

Remember, your goal at the outset is to identify target companies for investigation. If that step is performed correctly, it can save a lot of time and frustration. The 30 hours of due diligence does not start until you have identified the franchisor to begin researching.

The key questions to ask the target company:

- Is the franchise available in my area?

- Do I have the prerequisites required by the franchisor?

- Is the franchise in a growth mode?

- Is the industry growing?

- Does the franchise match my vision, skills and desires?

If those characteristics are solidly in place, then you are ready for your investigation to begin.

Chapter 10

Speaking With Franchisors: As You Study Them, They Study You

I keep six honest servicing-men (They taught me all I knew); Their names are What and Why and When and How and Where and Who.
– Rudyard Kipling

Franchising can be compared to a dating game, not a shopping trip. It is a two-way relationship, not a one-sided choice. As you are studying franchises, they're studying you!

For a moment, think back to your high school days—dare to be a bit nostalgic! With the high school dance approaching, you want to look your best. So you're out at the mall, surveying the latest fashions. You try on a few things, conclude you look pretty cool and make your purchase.

You've shopped!

But then there is the question of who is going to the dance with you. Is that a matter of simply deciding what suits you? Of course not! I don't care if you're the quarterback or class president; this decision is based on relationship building. The process may start with a choice of targets, but the decision is clearly bilateral.

Unfortunately, prospective franchisees sometimes enter into franchise investigation with the "shopper" mentality, assuming because they are the "buyer" that doors will swing wide open for them and franchisors will clamor for their attention.

In reality, buying a franchise is not like shopping at all. Finding the right franchise, something that meets all of your needs, is a more challenging process than looking and making a selection. It is more like dating in that the relationship has to make good sense for both parties. After all, the two parties are considering entering into a relationship that will last a number of years. It wouldn't make sense to legally bind yourself to an uncomfortable relationship.

The process of talking with franchisors involves a lot more than finding out their contact information, receiving brochures and getting a list of their franchisees.

And just like dating, it all starts with a positive first impression.

WHAT IS A FRANCHISOR REALLY LOOKING FOR?

Let's get into the franchisor's head so you can figure out the best way to present yourself to reputable franchisors.

The first thing to remember is that first impressions matter. In the two-way relationship of investigating a franchised business, a good first impression is very important. If you are truly serious about conducting a thorough investigation, solid introductory positioning is a useful first step. By positioning yourself properly at the beginning of the process, the franchisor is more likely to take your candidacy seriously and invest more time and energy with you.

Some of the first questions the franchisor will want you to answer are:

- What are the circumstances for wanting to explore entrepreneurship?

- Why do you think you will be a good business owner?

- What attracted you to seek more information about this particular offering?

- Do you have the financial capability to be successful in this franchise?

- What is your time frame for making a decision?

In almost all cases, the franchisor will start with a review of that set of questions so they can gain an understanding of your needs and whether there is a potential match with your goals and interests. They want to have confidence that they are proceeding with a viable candidate.

While the franchisor seeks candidates who are confident, they also look for good listeners. Most people examining businesses have some combination of an advanced education and strong work history, but even if your education includes a PhD or your resume includes a CEO title, you cannot bring a know-it-all approach to the exploration process.

One of the things you do NOT know is the system the franchisor has built and proven through extensive testing and measuring.

Let's say you have 20 years of experience as a house painter, and you're looking at a franchise related to painting. In a typical employment application process, you may want to impress the hiring manager with your expertise. But in a franchisor interview, taking charge of the discussion with a description of your vast painting knowledge and how you would do things is a serious red flag. It is considered a negative since you may not be open to following the franchisor's system.

Instead, your experience serves as "table stakes;" it's part of the value you bring to the table. What the franchisor brings is a strong, proven system of operating a business that is proven to be profitable—if followed.

The franchisor seeks candidates who will follow their prescribed due diligence system. Your degree of willingness to learn and follow their due diligence process will send a strong signal to the franchisor, and to yourself, about your willingness and ability to succeed in a proven system if you were to be awarded a franchise.

Don't forget that due diligence is a two-way street. The franchisor must assess whether you possess the right skill set for the business, whether that includes team management or sales experience. Early in the process they will also verify you indeed are interested in an available territory.

The franchisor also has to be certain your capital resources are sufficient for funding the business startup. You should expect to complete a detailed application form as an assurance that conducting a full-scale investigation is not a waste of your time or theirs.

Finally, don't be surprised if the franchisor uses a personality assessment tool to ascertain if you are a good match for their system. Different personalities are required for success in different franchises, so a personality profile is not used necessarily to screen you out, but it can help to identify areas where you would need extra support. You may be an extrovert who is perfectly comfortable in the marketing side of the business, but if your profile says administrative detail is a problem, the franchisor may ask about your commitment to outsourcing certain functions.

SURPRISE! THIS IS WHAT THE FRANCHISOR IS NOT LOOKING FOR!

The franchisor is NOT looking for an industry expert. In fact, some may resist it. A great example is in the highly successful Great Clips® franchise.

Great Clips does *not* look for franchisees with cosmetology licenses. Why? You can probably guess the obvious answer. They don't want to attract self-proclaimed experts who are interested only in the marketing brand, but then intend to "run things" their own way. As the saying goes, they want people to work "on" the business, not "in" it. Successful franchise systems work when franchisees are committed to following a proven model.

Once you have an appreciation for the franchisor's thinking and know the attributes they are seeking, you are positioned for entering their process.

UNDERSTANDING "SCREENS"

In a self-conducted franchise exploration, you may use a variety of direct methods of searching, most notably the Internet. When you discover interesting franchises, you may be inclined to use direct ways of contacting them, either by phone or through their websites.

Don't be surprised if you do not get a rapid response, or, in some cases, if you get no response at all. Franchisors may receive hundreds of contacts each day, so they employ screens as a way to economize their time and staff resources.

In some instances, you may not get a response at all because your area may not be under development by the company. If the person responsible for a franchisor's screening sees an area code or address that does not match their targets, they may simply ignore the request.

You can't assume every franchise company will get back to you, so don't be discouraged or take it personally if they don't.

If they do respond, be aware they may start the process with by having you complete a detailed application. Those who are new to the process may find the level of detail a bit disarming, but keep in mind the franchisor is also using this step as a screening method. And they're using it in two ways:

1) They want to know if you're truly qualified, financially and otherwise, to engage in a serious discussion of business ownership.

2) If you follow their direction and complete the application, it is a signal to the franchisor you may be a serious and system-focused candidate.

After you've passed through the basic screens, it is likely you will be contacted by either a sales representative from the company or an assistant who arranges appointments for the sales representative. Keep this contact in perspective. A contact from the sales rep simply means you have passed the initial screen and you are positioned for a discussion. You should not make an assumption about your viability as a franchisee or about the franchisor's viability as a match for you based on this contact.

LEARNING ABOUT THE OPPORTUNITY

If you are exploring independently, this is a crucial stage. It is the stage where you discover whether you are dealing with a reputable franchise. It is time to have your "radar system" fully activated.

If you are working with a quality franchise consulting organization, you will be introduced to franchisors that have passed the organizations internal due diligence. In this situation, the franchisors should be reputable. Even so, this is a good time to follow the advice of Former President of the United States, Ronald Reagan – "Trust, but verify".

Similarly, when franchise consultants refer prospects to a franchisor, the franchisor is confident the prospect has been pre-qualified and can proceed more quickly to the serious stages of discussion with the candidate.

In your independent investigation, you will engage in discussion with a franchise development officer for the franchise company. At the very start, you need to recognize this is a sales person for the company. But for quality franchisors, this particular sales person plays an interesting role as a go-between, in somewhat of an ambassador role.

With their sales hat on the development person will, of course, want to portray the franchise in a positive light and encourage the prospect to explore further. At the same time, they want to be sure they have a good match in the prospect, as the strength of the overall franchise system depends on attracting and retaining high-performing franchisees.

In the first conversation, the development person will walk you through the due diligence process. Although you'll find some differences among the various types of franchises, there are commonalities that should be consistent in due diligence.

You'll learn all of the foundational information about the franchise system, the fundamentals about how the business is structured and what products or services are provided. You'll then have the opportunity to speak with existing franchisees, a topic that will be covered extensively in the next chapter.

Along the way, you should have the opportunity to ask all the questions that are important to you. The franchise development officer may advise you in the first call that certain questions may be best answered at particular stages in the due diligence process. So don't feel the franchisor is being evasive if they do not instantly answer a question, but expect to hear some idea of when and how your question will be answered.

At some point in the process, either during or following your calls with franchisees, most franchisors will provide an opportunity to meet all their support personnel through a Discovery Day. Strong franchisors are proud of their team and want you to be exposed to them so you can enjoy a similar level of confidence. A Discovery Day allows you to get to know the people who will be important to your success. Some franchisors may even pay part of your expenses for a Discovery Day visit.

These steps are common among virtually all franchises, and the franchise development person who first interviews you will work with you to establish a timeline for conducting your due diligence. It is likely they will want to set a target date for arriving at a decision, with the target contingent upon how many hours per week you can dedicate to completing your investigation process.

The franchisor typically will not have a problem with the pace of your investigation, but they will want to be sure of your level of commitment in completing the entire process under their guidance. You will find them particularly sensitive about permitting validation calls with existing franchisees until they think you are ready. Existing franchisees are generous in volunteering to speak with potential franchisees. The franchisor will not want to waste the franchisee's valuable time by having them speak with prospects that are not serious about their research or a fit to the system.

At the end of the first call it must be evident to the franchise development representative that you are willing to commit yourself to the discovery process. If it is, in the next step you will receive a packet of promotional literature from the franchisor. Promotional materials may range from information about getting into the business to marketing materials that are actually used in the business, which should be high quality in both production and messaging.

Expect to talk with the franchise developer representative on multiple occasions, as their job is to act as both a guide and an information source. They are likely to start your discussion with company history and a vision for where the franchise is going. A great deal of time may be spent in explaining the marketing methods that are proven to be most effective for the company. If the franchise is a retail business, site selection will be a major priority.

The franchisor's development representative will also discuss the target demographics for their product or service, as market opportunity is commonly a significant area of focus for a prospective franchisee.

In the early stage of the discovery process, the franchisor will normally forward a copy of the Franchise Disclosure Document. They often set aside an entire call to review the document and to answer any questions you may have. These are important discussions, but they can only really happen after you have had several introductory calls with the franchisor.

WHAT IS THE FRANCHISE
DISCLOSURE DOCUMENT RECEIPT?

When you receive a copy of the Franchise Disclosure Document from the franchisor, you'll find a single-page receipt document attached to it to sign, date and return to the franchisor.

Sometimes people worry about it and wonder if it is something that will bind them to an obligation. In short, it doesn't. You do not need to worry about signing and returning the receipt. In fact, it's useful to promptly sign and return it for two reasons:

1) From the franchisor's perspective, it documents that the information in the Franchise Disclosure Document was provided to you. But more importantly, the signed receipt serves as a "trigger" mechanism for the franchise purchase to legally occur. The Franchise Disclosure Document must be in a prospective franchisee's possession for two weeks before any kind of deal can be legally consummated. This assures a careful, pressure-free purchase decision by the prospective franchisee.

2) The return of the receipt also indicates the prospect will conduct a serious review of the franchise and commitment to following systems.

STAYING ORGANIZED

A prospect's seriousness is critical at the outset of a franchise investigation. It's a process that demands focus and strong organization. It is common to feel overwhelmed by the amount of information that will pour in, particularly as you explore multiple franchises, and exploring multiple franchises simultaneously is important.

You should never research just one franchisor at a time. Even if you are exploring on your own, without the aid of a franchise consultant, it is beneficial to review three franchises simultaneously. This gives you the critical opportunity to compare and contrast various systems and approaches.

In fact, I recommend you set up three notebooks, one for each of the franchise companies you're reviewing. As a first step, write down the list of questions you will ask each franchisor and keep careful notes as you make contact with those companies.

Only write two or three questions per page, leaving plenty of room under each question. You will want to do this for two reasons. First, you will want to jot notes when the franchisor responds to particular questions. Second, you'll want to leave space after the franchisor's answers so you can compare them later to the responses existing franchisees give you to the same questions.

This is called cross-validation and it is an important step in helping you gain a stronger understanding of the business.

SUMMARY

The key to success in this stage of your franchise investigation is to focus on the following:

Carefully following the "discovery process" laid out by the franchisor. Typically it is well tested over time and is designed to culminate in a well informed decision. Good franchisors want you to make your decision with eyes wide open. Make sure all your questions and concerns are fully addressed. If there are gaps, or if you feel certain topics are being avoided, those are red flags that should cause concern.

As you progress through the process under the guidance of the franchisor, keep in mind you should not see your role as that of a "buyer." Remember, the franchisor has just as much at stake and is carefully performing due diligence on you as a prospect.

If you are perceived as being overly demanding or pushy in the due diligence process, the franchisor may take that as a sign you may not be manageable within the parameters of the system, or that you may be thinking of acquiring a franchise and then doing your own thing. Franchisors admire entrepreneurial spirit; however, they look for a balance of traits in their franchisees—including discipline.

Many good franchisors will not allow prospects to become franchisees without assurance that they have successfully completed the learning process. A good franchisor is looking for a win-win outcome, so they want to make sure a prospect has all of their questions answered before moving forward to dialogue with franchisees.

Chapter 11

Validating With Franchisees

LEARNING is not attained by chance. It must be sought
for with ardor and attended to with diligence.
— Abigail Adams

SPEAKING WITH FRANCHISEES

Most people underestimate the importance of speaking with franchisees. You simply cannot begin to really understand a franchise system until you spend time on the phone with the critical sources of information known as franchisees. Not only do you need to speak with a good number of franchisees, but you also need to vary the types of franchisees and carefully consider how you approach questioning them.

It is important to realize that franchisees are not required to speak with you. It is not a part of their contractual obligations under the franchise agreement, and they do not receive any compensation for speaking with you.

Typically, franchisees speak with you because they appreciate the fact that others helped them when they were examining franchising and that well-informed candidates make better decisions. This, of course, results in better franchisees being added to the team. If a franchisor is able to aggregate enough great franchisees, the result is a great franchise system, which benefits everyone. In many ways, the franchisees are the barometer through which you can honestly measure the success of a franchise system; however, this barometer only works if you know how to read it.

SECURING PERMISSION TO CALL FRANCHISEES

Securing permission to speak with the franchisees in a system usually requires a little effort. Before providing access to the franchisees, the franchisor is responsible for ensuring you have the fundamental requirements to be a successful franchisee and have a foundation of knowledge. This step assures that your contacts with existing franchisees will be productive and will not waste time. These fundamentals, at a minimum, include the correct skill sets, a positive approach and financial capability. The franchisor also wants to make sure you have a basic understanding of the business model. Starting the franchisee conversation with, "What does this franchise do?" would be less than impressive. A quality franchisor wants to educate you on the basics of their business system prior to allowing you to access the franchisee system.

Once you have completed the introductory steps and are ready to begin calling franchisees, you will need a complete list of franchisees. You can find this in the Exhibits section of the Franchise Disclosure Document. Unfortunately, depending on the publication date, the list in the Franchise Disclosure Document can be dated by a year or more. Always ask the franchisor for an updated list including all contact information for the franchisees. They should be able to email this to you in short order. If you have completed the initial steps and the franchisor is still unwilling to provide you with a full and updated list of the franchisees, you may want to reconsider your interest in the franchise system.

When you call a franchisee, it is imperative you quickly share with them the fact that you are a valid candidate for the given franchise. Most franchise systems employ some sort of password or validation system in order to ensure this is the case. Without a password or validation system, the franchisee would not know if you are a real candidate or a competitor intent on nosing around in their business. Without the password, the franchisee is not likely to want to speak with you.

WHICH FRANCHISEES SHOULD I CALL?

Let's say you have passed the initial screens, gone through the initial steps and understand the foundation of the franchise. Now it is time to speak with franchisees and determine which franchise owners to call.

As you look at a franchise system, you need to realize it is like any other group of people. The top 20% of the franchisees should be doing VERY well – they are the stars. The middle 60% should be making a nice living – working the business everyday, putting in the time and making it work. The bottom 20% of the franchisees are not doing that well – they are the ones who are normally looking to leave the systems or are holding a side job while trying to hold their business together. You need to know this because now you are going to be calling all three categories of franchisees, and you need to know with which category you are speaking. There are a number of strategies you may want to employ at this stage. I suggest you use some, or preferably, all of the following:

▶ The best in the system

Ask the franchisor to share with you who the leaders are in the system. These are the people that are doing a great job. They are growing a big business and playing a leadership role within the franchise community. You want to speak with them for a number of reasons. You want to know what success means in a given system. "How big is big?" You need to make sure your definition is the same as the person you're questioning. One franchisee may be thrilled with a $100,000 net profit, while another may consider it disappointing.

Second, you want to know what type of people they are. Are they like you? If they are like you, is your level of success likely to be similar? Finally, you want to know what it takes to be the best within the system. Could you see yourself building the type of business they built?

▶ Old vs. new

It is very important to realize that the type of questions and discussion you have with a new franchisee are likely to be different from the discussion you would have with an experienced franchisee. The older franchisee has a historical perspective to the system. They have seen the evolution that naturally occurs within a system. An older franchisee can tell you about what it is like to own the business for an extended period of time and whether it gets easier or harder. At the same time, the newer franchisee can tell you more about the training program and the opening support. They have more recently gone through the opening cycle and the information is fresh in mind. The more seasoned franchisee, even if they remember what the opening cycle was like, may not be alert to the fact that the opening cycle has probably changed several times. A good franchisor will continually change and improve the training and opening support system to both reflect learning and to respond to market forces and expectations. Be sure to ask the right questions to the right franchisees.

▶ *Franchisees who are selling or closing*

It is fair to ask a franchisor for the name of franchisees that have their businesses for sale or are considering closing their franchise. Every franchisee system has franchises that are for sale. This is normal and expected. The critical question you need answered is "Why?"

- Is the business for sale because the owner is retiring and selling out at a profit?

- Is the business for sale because the franchisee does not have the skills to be successful?

- Is the business for sale because of health issues?

- Is the business for sale because of change in local or national consumer patterns?

- Is the business for sale because of a failure of the franchisor's system?

- Is the business for sale because the franchisee wants to hike the Appalachian Trail?

Keep digging until you feel you really understand the reason for the sale.

Generally, you will find the driver for the sale to be one of the following:

1) Proactive desire to sell due to external circumstances.

2) Failure of the business due to franchisee's inability or unwillingness to follow the system.

    or

3) A bad system that cannot drive success at the franchisee level.

In the first example, if the business is being sold to allow the owner to move forward to the next stage of their life, it can be a good thing, especially if they have had a good run and will be selling at a profit.

In the second example, you need to ask yourself if you are like this person. Do you have the right skills to be successful and will you be willing to follow the franchisor's systems? If you answer, "Yes, I am like this person and would have the same approach to the business," be very careful about moving forward. If you answer "No, I am not like this person and would not have the same approach," simply add the information to your learning and keep moving forward.

In the third example, be very careful. The reason you are getting into a franchise is to reduce your business risk. If the franchise cannot do this, it has very little value. In this type of situation, you will usually find a high percentage of franchisees that have their business for sale.

▶ *Franchisees who are similar to you*

Every franchise system is filled with people from a wide variety of backgrounds and with a wide variety of expectations. Target franchisees who are similar to you. This may mean income expectations, education, skills, personality, drive, experience, market type, age, sex, marital status, etc. These franchisees most likely faced the same challenges you may face and will be a great support network to you as you grow the business. The best way to identify these franchisees is to ask the franchisor for assistance. The franchisor typically records information about the franchisees, such as work history, their education, etc. and can give you some guidance regarding who you should target.

▶ Random calls

Of course, you need to make random calls in order to properly gauge the overall health of the system. Regrettably, some franchisors may promote only the best franchisees and try to keep you from speaking to less successful franchisees. Random calls will give you a good idea as to the general feeling and health of the system, and a strong franchisor will encourage you to speak with any of their franchisees.

▶ The closest franchisee

This is an area that requires significant **caution**. The first thing most candidates want to do is to call the franchisee just down the road. The problem with this method is that discussions with franchisees are intended to be unbiased, but when you speak with the franchisee down the road, you risk getting biased information. Why? Because most franchisees either believe having a franchisee down the road will help their business or hurt their business. Most franchisees expect one day to buy the territory down the road or to sell their own business to the owner down the road. The real challenge is that you don't know which it is. The information may be biased and you may not get an honest read on the franchise.

Another risk you take in talking with the closest neighboring franchisee is you may lose out on a great opportunity because you have alerted the more experienced franchisee that the territory may be purchased. Let's say you are interested in opening a food franchise and you call the nearby three-year franchisee. Your call may be a reminder that a contiguous territory is available and potentially lucrative. In turn, the experienced franchisee may call the franchisor and immediately engage in purchase discussions without any delay.

The franchisor's reaction? Think about it. If you have the choice between an experienced, proven franchisee versus a newcomer who will need to learn the ropes of the business, what would your choice be?

So if you wish to speak with the franchisee down the road, do this at the end of your calls, when other views have shaped your decision. Speak with ten other franchisees first and then speak with the franchisee down the road. You will be better positioned to "interpret" that franchisee's comments, and always keep in mind calling the closest franchise can, in some cases, lead to loss of opportunity.

Also keep in mind that not everyone will be having a good day when you contact them. Even the best franchisees within a system have down days and, conversely, poorly performing franchisees have good days. This process is about averages. Your first call may be with the only happy franchisee within the system or it may be with the only unhappy franchisee within the system. Through multiple calls, you will learn about the norms and be in a better position to set your expectations.

THE EXCEPTIONS

Some high growth franchises have an imbalance between interested parties and current franchisees. Let's imagine the system is three years old and has 20 franchisees. Only a four or five franchisees may have more than one or two years of experience. If the system is really taking off, there may be 50 people going through the due diligence process concurrently.

It does not take a lot of math to realize that if every candidate called those same four or five franchisees individually, the franchisees would not have time to successfully run and grow their business. In this situation, the franchisor will often employ a conference call system. You will be invited on a number of conference calls along with a group of other prospective franchisees.

This can have advantages and disadvantages. The advantage is you will not only get to ask your questions, but also get to hear questions other candidates ask. You will learn things you may not have thought to ask. These calls can be dynamic and truly enlightening, or on the other hand, they can be quite boring. It all depends on who is on the line. The best thing you can do for yourself is to sit in on as many conference calls as possible and have a few questions prepared for each call. If there are a number of folks on the call, everyone will get a chance to ask a few questions. If there are only a couple of prospects on the call, take advantage of the situation and ask as many of your questions as you can.

The disadvantage to this process is you may not be able to get down to the level of detail you require. Your strategy here is to learn as much as you can on the conference calls, thereby respecting the franchisees' time. If you are at the end of the process and have a few additional questions before you can make a "go/no go" decision, and the conference call format is not appropriate for your questions, go back to the franchisor. Ask them to set up a call for you with the franchisees of your choice. Usually, if you have spent enough time on the conference calls and have been otherwise diligent, the franchisor will be accommodating and help you get directly in touch with the target franchisees.

EMAILING QUESTIONS

Some people prefer to forward questions via email. Although email may be useful to set up a time for a meeting, emailing a list of questions does not usually work. Most franchisees prefer to speak to someone, as opposed to sitting at a computer typing out responses so you tend to get a low hit rate.

You also miss important information. Many times *how* something is said is more important than *what* is said. You do not want to miss the finer intonation found in a conversation. At the same time, the answer to one question may bring up another related question. If you prepare well for a conversation (interview), then you can get a wealth of information.

ORGANIZING YOUR QUESTIONS

To get maximum benefit from the calls (and to respect the franchisees' time), you need to be well prepared for the call. This means having a list of questions you want to cover during the call. I suggest having a list of questions that is not only comprehensive but also sorted by topic and prioritized from the most important to the least important questions. Most often, the list is much longer than you will have time to cover during the call. That's why it is important to ask the franchisee how much time they have for the call and then manage your questions accordingly.

As your calls progress, you will find that the questions you ask will change, based on your comfort and knowledge. If you have asked the same question three times and each time you received exactly the same answer, you may wish to move on to other questions. If you ask the question three times and each time you get a different answer, you may need to dig further. The key is to ask the question often enough to feel comfortable that you fully understand the response.

I have developed a starter list of questions you may want to ask. These questions cover the primary topics, but the list is only a start. You will create the complete list of questions. The full list will be driven by the franchise system that you are evaluating and will expand and grow as you learn more. To download this list of questions, go to the resource section of www.educatedfranchisee.com.

KEY POINT

As you ask questions, be very careful to get past "yes/no" answers. For example, "Are you doing well in your business?" is a yes/no question. This question tells you next to nothing. The key is to follow-up the first question with, "Why is that?" By doing this you will gather great information and your due diligence will come to life.

The more a franchisee likes you, the more time and detail they will give you when you speak with them. If they don't like you, they may be short with you and downplay the business, thinking you do not fit the personality of the franchise system. Use your best relationship building skills. This process should deliver great information, energize you and be a lot of fun. Remember, if you become a franchisee, many of the franchisees you call will become close personal friends that in some cases last a lifetime.

SUMMARY

With focused calls you will begin to get a sense of whether you fit the "personality" of the system. Some systems are serious, some fun, some aggressive. When you talk with owners, you will get a sense of the system's personality. When you find a system where your personality is a match, you will feel a sense of home and a sense of family.

Be sure to structure your franchisee calls carefully. Choose the right franchisees to call and ask them the right questions. Be sure to listen intently, not only to the answer, but also to how the answer is presented. Additionally, remember to validate the system, not an individual franchisee's performance.

Most of all, be sure to have fun with this process. This is one of the most enjoyable and enlightening aspects of your due diligence process. You should emerge from these calls with a strong sense of the company, great information and positive energy.

Chapter 12

The Key To Building Your Financial Model: Asking The Right Questions!

He who asks a question is a fool for five minutes;
he who does not ask a question remains a fool forever.
– Chinese Proverb

Earnings are almost always one of the highest priority topics for the prospective franchisee. It's also an area where some of the biggest mistakes can be made during the process of interviewing existing franchisees.

Strange as it may sound, mistakes often stem from too much focus on the bottom line, or what a potential franchisee *thinks* is the bottom line. In an examination of a franchisee's financial picture, an over-emphasis on the bottom line profit number can be misleading, and even dangerous. Here's why.

The bottom line is more a function of tax treatment than profitability!

Most people, when beginning to learn about the P&L of a particular franchise, go about the process incorrectly. They ask "bottom line" questions such as:

- "What is your salary?"

- "What is your break even?"

- "What is your profit?"

These questions are well intentioned, but the answer does not educate—it misleads.

When you ask, "What is your salary?" you are really trying to determine, "What do I get to take home?" You are trying to understand the entire business by asking one bottom line question. But neither the question nor the bottom-line number provide enough information.

Take the following simple example. If you ask a franchisee, "What is your salary?" The franchisee may say $200,000 per year, or they may say $0, i.e. no salary at all. Which is the better business? The reality may be that it is impossible to tell. The person taking $200K in salary per year may be losing money and near bankruptcy. Remember the Dot Coms? They took home millions in salary and never made any money. On the other hand, the person taking no salary may be a billionaire. Look at Steve Jobs, the CEO of Apple, or Larry Page and Sergey Brin, the co-founders of Google. They all receive a salary of $1 / year. You need to look deeper.

The better question to examine is, "How do I make money in this business?"

Many of us, through years of corporate conditioning, train our sights on the bottom line number, but we have to remember that the small business owner makes money many different ways. The full P&L is the only way to fully understand how the business makes money.

As you know by now, the franchisee can be the best source of unbiased information on earnings, but *how* you structure your questions will be critical when it comes to gathering useful information.

Franchisees, when answering the questions, may be honest and unbiased—from their perspective. But it may be the case that neither the prospect nor the franchisee realize they are comparing apples and oranges.

In order to better understand how to make money in a particular franchise business, you need to refocus on what I call "Owner benefit." Owner benefit is achieved in a number of different ways. A franchisee realizes an ***owner benefit*** because:

- An owner is able to take a certain amount of their profit and put it into a retirement account much more aggressively than you can as an employee.

- An owner can take money from the company as a distribution, without having to pay social security taxes.

- An owner can legally pass a number of personal business expenses through the business.

- An owner can attribute significant "costs of doing business," such as child care, as a business expense.

And that's just to name a few of the ways to realize owner benefit. You can find many more. If you wish to really study the wide variety of ways to structure a P&L, take some time to read *Loopholes of the Rich* by Diane Kennedy, CPA. This is a great book that will open your eyes to the amazing power of business ownership and wealth creation. Look at how the P&L is built: from the top, down. That's the only way to fully understand, "How do I make money in this business?"

For your interviews with existing franchisees, prepare some easy questions:

- What are the line items on your P&L?

- How does each line item work?

First, you can simply ask the franchisor to send the list of line items. They are legally able to send you that in a blank format. You will have to plug in the numbers. Where do you get the numbers to plug in? From the existing franchisees.

Franchisees can, and typically will, share P&L information, whether revenue or expense. On the other hand, unless the franchisor has a complete P&L in Item 19 of the Franchise Disclosure Document (see Chapter 7), the franchisor will be prohibited from discussing any expense or revenue number that would lead a person to build a P&L or set an expectation they can earn a particular amount of money in the franchised business. Even if the franchisor has a solid P&L in the Franchise Disclosure Document, you still want to speak with enough franchisees to gain a solid understanding of each line item.

Here is a simplified P&L example that will serve as an illustration of how miscommunication can occur. We'll examine the model below.

First, it's important to make the distinction between how a typical employee views a P&L vs. how a business owner looks at the same financial statement.

THE IMPORTANCE OF OWNER BENEFIT

Many people understand profit-and-loss statements. They may have studied them in school and may be conversant in corporate P&L reviews; however, when most people try to translate their knowledge to the business owner's perspective, they may experience a gap in their knowledge.

As employees, people readily understand the construct that says they get paid a salary, the government takes out taxes and what's left is take-home pay.

$$Salary - Taxes = Pay$$

As a result, when they envision what their P&L might be as a business owner, that same construct follows them. Their first thought is often, "What salary am I going to pay myself?" They see the same "S – T = P" formula operating in the salaries line of their own P&L. When you do that, you are missing the most important part of business ownership: owner benefit.

In some cases **owner benefit** can be seen as synonymous with profit. The big difference is that owner benefit can be realized in different lines of the P&L, not just the profit line. For those of you who are accountants, please keep in mind that this is not an accounting term, it is a descriptive. It describes _all_ the benefit an owner can derive from a business, regardless of when and how the benefit is taken. Other terms that sometimes are used are "Total Owners Discretionary Profit" or "EBITDA plus Add backs."

Owner benefit is the amount of funds the business owner takes from the business if all tax treatments are stripped away. The owner can take compensation from the expense line of the P&L, or the owner can take compensation from the profit line. There are many ways to realize owner benefit. The business owner has the latitude to determine how excess capital will be utilized.

The key point about managing your own P&L is that you decide, in accordance with the rules of the game established by the Generally Accepted Accounting Principals (GAAP) and the IRS, where to account for the expenses of operating the business. Because the government

ledge related to P&L and financials. If you can add and subtract,
ill be able to use this approach.

STEP 1

e a list of the line items on the P&L. What are line items? The line
are the categories of income and expense on the left side of the
In other words, where does the money come from and where does

Gross Income	$ 200,000	
Expenses		
Labor	$ 50,000	25%
Marketing	$ 50,000	25%
Communication	$ 10,000	5%
Auto	$ 40,000	20%
Travel and meeting	$ 10,000	5%
Training	$ 8,000	4%
Daycare	$ 5,000	3%
Profit sharing plan	$ 20,000	10%
Rent	$ 10,000	5%
Total expenses	$ 203,000	
Net Profit (Loss)	$ (3,000)	- 2%

efore speaking with any franchisees, try to guess what the line
might be for the franchise you're considering. Don't worry if you
et the full list of line items correct; just get a good start and then
e franchisees to assist you in completing the list. Some franchisors
e you the line items if you ask. For a home-based service business,
safely assume there must be: sales, marketing, communication,
d travel. If the franchisor does not provide the line items, the list
s a good enough starting point. Start with this list and simply
e franchisee, "I am trying to build a P&L and have a few line
lready listed. Could you confirm these are correct and let me
I have missed any?"

ery franchisee can effectively answer this question because they
income and pay the bills. By the time you are finished speaking
e franchisee about line items, you will find that a number of items

wants you to succeed—they want you to grow an know

the deck is stacked in your favor from a tax stand¡ you v

A P&L CASE STUDY

And now, for illustration purposes, let's review a ş Crea

Assumptions for this business: items
P&L.
it go?

- Small business

- No full time employees

- Works from home

- They employ a skilled CPA

This is the current P&L.

Gross Income	$ 200,000
Expenses	
Labor	$ 50,000
Marketing	$ 50,000
Communication	$ 10,000
Auto	$ 40,000
Travel and meeting	$ 10,000
Training	$ 8,000
Daycare	$ 5,000
Profit sharing plan	$ 20,000
Rent	$ 10,000
Total expenses	**$ 203,000**
Net Profit (Loss)	**$ (3,000)**

If you ask, "What is your profit?" the ansv auto a;
you ask, "What is your break even?" the answ(above
business does not break even." You can easil ask th
Based on the prospect's *bottom line* financial ā items ;
business and a bad business opportunity. know i

Now let's look at the P&L from a *top down* Ev
is a small, home-based service business with no receive
a very good CPA. I am going to give you a top with th
help you to analyze this business regardless of

are never discussed because the franchisee knows that these items are not "business related expenses." The line items will now look like this:

Gross Income
Expenses
Labor
Marketing
Communication
Auto
Travel and meeting
Training
Daycare
Profit sharing plan
Rent
Total expenses
Net Profit (Loss)

Note the Daycare expenses and Retirement program line item will both drop out because they are not business-related expenses. They are simply ways to structure your P&L so as to honestly reduce your taxes.

STEP 2

Now you need to learn a little bit about each item. Your question to the franchisee is, "Do you mind if I ask you about each line item so I can more fully understand the business?"

▶ *Cost of Labor*

How many employees do you have? Do you track this as a percent of sales or is it a flat rate? (Remember, salary is a word that only applies to employees. As a business owner, you benefit from the profit of the corporation, which, of course, is what you want.)

▶ *Cost of Marketing*

What do you expect your marketing costs to be? Is this a flat monthly fee or it is a percentage of gross sales?

▶ Communication

How much do you spend per month in business related communication expenses? How does that break down?

▶ Auto

Considering this is a home-based business, how many business related miles do you drive per month?

▶ Travel and Meeting

How many trips do you have to take per year for business?

▶ Training

How much additional training are you required to take? How much do you think is an appropriate amount?

▶ Rent

Do you need an outside office? How many square feet? How much do you pay per square foot?

When you finish the interviews with the franchisees, the new P&L looks like this:

Gross Income	$ 200,000	
Expenses		
Labor	$ 10,000	5%
Marketing	$ 50,000	25%
Communication	$ 8,000	4%
Auto	$ 30,000	15%
Travel and meeting	$ 10,000	2%
Training	$ 4,000	2%
Rent	$ -	0%
Total expenses	**$ 105,000**	
Net Profit (Loss)	**$ 95,000**	**48%**

So where did the rest of the P&L go? Why does it look so different now?

We separated the real, business related expenses from the many other expenses that people often put on their P&L. If you were able to fully break down *all* the expenses found on the previous, tax-based P&L, it would look like this:

Gross Income	$ 200,000	
Expenses		
Labor	$ 10,000	5%
Marketing	$ 50,000	25%
Communication	$ 8,000	4%
Auto	$ 30,000	15%
Travel and meeting	$ 10,000	2%
Training	$ 4,000	2%
Rent	$ 3,000	0%
Total expenses	$ -	
Net Profit (Loss)	$ 95,000	**48%**

Owner Benefit Distribution		
Salary to owner	$ 40,000	20%
Children's cell phones (they help at business)	$ 2,000	1%
Travel with family (and business meeting)	$ 6,000	3%
Profit sharing plan contribution (retirement)	$ 20,000	10%
Training for new business idea	$ 5,000	3%
Daycare expense	$ 5,000	3%
Rent of your home office	$ 10,000	5%
Multi purpose auto miles	$ 10,000	5%
Total owner benefit	$ 98,000	

This business produces $98,000 per year in owner benefit. The owner has chosen to take $40,000 home as salary, place $20,000 in a retirement plan, and pass the remaining $38,000 through the business as a legal expense.

By using this *Top Down* approach to understanding the basics of the P&L, you have gathered honest information about how the business really works and have naturally separated the real business expenses from the expenses that are often found on a P&L due to tax reasons.

OTHER ADVANTAGES TO A TOP DOWN APPROACH

There are some additional advantages to using the *Top Down* approach to understanding the financial information. One advantage is when you ask five franchisees the same question, "What are your marketing costs?" you are going to get five different answers. One may say 25%, another 28%, a third may say 21%, and so on. Once you gather this type of information, you can begin to average the information and determine highs and lows. In order words, you can really begin to understand the possibilities as they relate to the franchise.

In addition, you will more accurately build your business plan for your new business. A quality franchisor is going to want you to have a solid understanding of how, when and why the business makes money. This approach will allow you to better understand the potential realities of business ownership.

FOR THE SEASONED ACCOUNTING PROFESSIONAL

Often, when I work with seasoned accounting professionals, I hear a hint of boredom in their voices when I review this information. Please understand this approach is just as important for you as it is for the balance of the prospective business owners. As an accountant, you know exactly what you mean when you ask for the "Months to Cash Flow Break Even" or EBITDA following GAAP. The problem is that most of the franchisees you speak with are more focused on growing their business than formalizing their financial statements. They don't have exact answers for you and, even if they did, they may fail to share with you a critical aspect of their treatment of salaried income. By using the above mentioned approach, you will come away with great information that will allow you to build a solid P&L that will enable you to fully understand the business.

SUMMARY

Speaking with franchisees is one of the most important parts of your due diligence process. By targeting the right franchisees, asking the best questions, and being organized and focused you can gather a tremendous amount of information in a short period of time.

Remember to use the top down approach to analyzing the P&L, and do NOT hesitate to ask questions of the franchisor and franchisees. The more detailed the questions, the more likely it is you will fully understand the business.

You are not applying for a job. Both you and the franchisor are mutually determining whether it makes sense to enter into a business relationship. The franchisor will be much more impressed with a solid list of questions from a prospect than by a complete absence of questions.

Chapter 13

Financing Your Business

If you would know the value of
money, go try to borrow some.
— Benjamin Franklin

Franchising attracts seasoned entrepreneurs who understand and appreciate the value of a proven operating system. Franchising also attracts, more so than other forms of business entry, many first-time business owners. These may be people who want to leave a corporate career behind, with either positive or negative motivations for seeking a new career path. They may be people who have always had an entrepreneurial flair and joined corporate America to save money to start a business.

Whichever the case and regardless of your personal financial situation, the subject of financing must be addressed early in the process. For the same reason that a search for a new home sensibly begins with a pre-qualification for a home loan, you should know what you can afford and how comfortable you will be investing in a business. The last thing you want to do is identify a fantastic opportunity, get really pumped up about it, and then discover you are either delayed or shut out completely in terms of financing.

As mentioned earlier, it will be one of the key qualifying questions a franchisor will want to know. The franchisor is just as interested in knowing how qualified you are as you are in knowing how much the franchise costs.

As a prospective franchisee it is very important you fully explore both *how* and *how much*.

In fact, the "how much" question—that is, the price tag for the franchise—has the same potential for misunderstanding as the bottom line question discussed in Chapter 12. Due to financing alternatives, you may find a business that demands a $200K total investment may be more affordable from a cash point of view than one necessitating a $100K total investment. If your first question to a franchisor is, *"How much?"* it may send the negative signal that you are short on capital and risk averse. Both are bad signals to send in the first several minutes of starting a relationship.

In addition, if the only figure you know is the price, how do you know whether the price is right? I urge you to know your general investment range before you start to explore franchises. This may include speaking with franchise financing companies prior to approaching franchisors. This can save you both time and effort. It will also allow you to demonstrate to the franchisor that you are serious and prepared to discuss the franchised business opportunity.

To embark on a productive study, it's best to be armed with some basic information about the kinds of money available for business investment. In other words, it's a good idea to *pre-qualify* yourself.

TWO KINDS OF MONEY: DEBT AND EQUITY

Fundamentally, there are two types of money available to potentially finance your business entry: debt and equity.

Debt is money you have to pay back. It's money that has been given to you on a loan, usually secured by some sort of collateral. Over time, it has to be returned to the lender, and returned with interest. It is the same type of relationship as a home loan and your arrangement with the banker.

Debt financing generally requires you offer something of value as collateral. Typically that would be property you own. There are varieties of debt financing alternatives available, and we'll get into those shortly.

Equity financing does not have to be repaid in a traditional sense. Equity financing involves someone giving you money in exchange for an ownership stake in the business. On one hand, that is a nice method because you do not have the cash flow concern that comes with paying back that debt. Of course, you have to keep in mind that you must give a certain portion of your profits to the equity financing partner, so you must be able to come to terms with continuing that division of profits.

There are also alternatives that combine debt and equity financing. One example of this type of hybrid would be where debt financing is offered and has to be repaid, but instead of traditional collateralization, equity ownership is given. As you speak with more creative financiers, you will find there are a number of ways to structure financing, but regardless of the approach there are a few rules of thumb.

Here are some of rules of thumb to keep in mind:

- **No free rides:** Nobody will just give you money because you have a brilliant idea or good business credentials. If someone is going to give you money, they are going to demand something in return, whether it is collateralization and interest or an equity stake in the business. Knowing that, it is important to consider what is fair up front, write it down and then be willing to live by it. This is true if you are borrowing money from a bank or from your Great Aunt Edna.

- **Manage your cash flow:** If you decide to go with debt financing, which many people do, you have to keep in mind your business loan requires regular payment. In fact, you should look at investing in a business the same way you would look at buying a house and making a mortgage payment. These payments create a negative cash flow, so you have to be prepared for that. As you make additional investments in your business, the debt will grow—and so will the interest.

- **Guard your cash position:** As businesses and families grow, unexpected expenses occur. Whether it is a vehicle that breaks or braces for your child's teeth, make sure you do not run out of available cash. Set up lines of credit before opening the business so if you need additional cash for unexpected expenses, you will have access to the needed funds. Of course, debt service and personal living expenses should be worked into your cash flow projections

- **Don't over-invest:** Be careful if you are considering investing more than 50% of your net worth. In the early days of most businesses, they have a negative cash flow. This means you will not be able to pull money out of the business. So you have to make sure you are positioned from a cash flow standpoint to withstand the startup phase of your business.

DEBT FINANCING OPTIONS

▶ SBA loans

The SBA, Small Business Administration, provides a wonderful service to the small business sector, but the SBA's role is not what many people envision when they think about governmental entity financing.

It's a misnomer to think of the SBA as a lender. While the agency is instrumental in the approval of many loans for startup businesses, in most cases, they play a secondary support role. The SBA endorses a list of bank and non-bank lenders, and it is the participating lenders that have the direct lending relationship with the successful business loan applicants. The SBA most often acts as a loan guarantor for the lender.

The business owner applies for a loan with the SBA-approved lender. The lender takes its customary collateralization position with the borrower to protect the lender's interests to the greatest extent possible. The SBA is the guarantor of that loan in the event of a default by the borrower. In other words, the bank is assured of additional protection by the SBA. Without SBA backing, many lenders would chose not to offer commercial loans to startup businesses.

The SBA also pre-approves many franchisors. It is a mark of quality when a franchisor is an SBA-approved business. That is a sign the franchise's business plan is sound and has a proven track record. One of the most positive aspects of dealing with an SBA-approved franchise is the financing process is somewhat expedited. That is an important factor when you've completed your investigation and you're excited about getting started. You don't want to run into bureaucratic roadblocks at the time when you're eager to get started. If you wish to view a list of SBA approved companies, please visit www.educatedfranchisee.com.

You must keep in mind that your credit rating and collateralization must be in good shape, and you must submit a convincing business plan to the lender in order to receive financing. As of the writing of this book, the interest rate is often 2 to 2.5 points above prime, with anywhere from 20 to 30 percent down payment required from the borrower. So for a $100,000 business, the bank would expect you to have $20,000-$30,000 in cash to invest, with the loan being for the remainder.

Although you are able to manage an SBA loan process directly with the lender, I would strongly suggest you consider the advantages of having a specialist working on your behalf. Many brokers are experts at knowing which lenders prefer which types of loans and they can greatly expedite the loan submittal and approval process.

More information on reputable financing companies can be found in the resource section of www.educatedfranchisee.com.

▶ *HELOC*

Establishing a HELOC (Home Equity Line of Credit) is one of the most popular ways of financing a franchise startup. Since homes are the most common form of collateralization for most loans, it makes good sense for many people to use the equity in their home for financing, particularly those who have substantial equity in their homes.

As of this writing, the cost of a HELOC was right around prime, if not a quarter-point below prime. There is a substantial difference in the cost of this financing. An SBA loan may cost thousands of dollars per application, but often you get can a HELOC for little or no money from your mortgage lender or bank.

Even though HELOC's are available if you have equity in your home, I would suggest you establish your HELOC before leaving your current employment. It is possible to secure a HELOC after leaving your current employer, but your borrowing power is significantly improved when you are employed. You will generally get a better rate and a larger HELOC prior to leaving your employment.

Finally, because these types of loans are exceptionally common, the total time from application to approval is often a week to ten days.

▶ *F&F financing*

While some view F&F financing, which simply refers to friends & family, with trepidation, this method is actually quite popular and is less worrisome when viewed from the proper perspective.

Skeptics may view F&F as a matter of appealing to Aunt Tillie to part with her life savings. That's not what we're talking about here. F&F does not involve an emotional appeal for loved ones to risk their life savings.

Instead, F&F is simply offering people who know and trust you a way of investing their money and entering into a business relationship that can be an attractive alternative to putting their money into the stock market or another investment.

Just as it is common for someone to require co-signers on a credit card or auto loan application, this type of financing could involve asking someone to be a co-signer on a loan, but with one difference. You promise to reward the friend or family member with an appropriate return for investing with you. You could also structure a straight collateralized loan that you would repay or you could offer equity in your business.

The key is to make sure you structure the relationship as an arm's length transaction. That is, don't view the transaction as informal. Go to the extent of having a lawyer assist you in structuring the loan. A lawyer will ask you and your financing partner a series of questions designed to help you set your expectations and then a document will be drafted to formalize the relationship. By using this approach, you will both be comfortable regarding opportunity and risk.

▶ Equipment loan

This form of financing may raise a question mark in your mind, until you place it in a more common frame of reference. A car loan is the most common form of equipment financing. An equipment loan is one in which the collateralization of the loan is in the actual item being financed.

Many franchises, perhaps as many as half, involve some sort of major equipment purchases, such as vehicles. Restaurants tend to have equipment loans attached to them, with pizza ovens and fryers being the most common items requiring financing.

▶ Signature loans

If you have exceptionally good credit and significant net worth, a bank may give you a loan simply because of the perceived low risk in doing so. In fact, if it's a bank that already enjoys a solid relationship with you, they may be inclined to give you a loan based on nothing more than "your good name," for the sake of earning future business with you.

The relationship is similar in some ways to getting a credit card. If your credit rating and net worth are strong, you will attract lenders willing to do business with you. These loans tend to be in the $10K to $20K range.

▶ Business loan

Business loans without an SBA guarantee are unlikely for new business startups; however, in the instance of buying an existing franchise business with a proven record, you may be able to qualify for a business loan. As long as you are able to demonstrate a proven cash flow, business assets to collateralize the loan and the ability to cover the debt payments, you may be eligible for this type of financing.

EQUITY FINANCING OPTIONS

The definition of equity financing sounds both simple and appealing. It is money that is put into the business in a cash format and does NOT have to be repaid. At first blush, what could be more appealing than that?!

Frankly, it depends on how much ownership you have to give up for the cash infusion.

And the simplest form of cash infusion is just that: CASH!

▶ Cash

If you take cash from whatever source: stocks, bonds or savings, and put it into the business, that's equity financing. You own the business outright. You are basically serving as your own venture capitalist. You retain all ownership in return for your cash investment in the business.

That, of course, is the core definition of cash financing, no matter where the cash comes from.

▶ *Self-directed retirement rollover*

This form of cash financing, sometimes referred to as ESOP (Entrepreneurial Stock Ownership Program), has become more popular, particularly with the influx of former corporate employees entering the entrepreneurship arena.

In this situation, instead of using your liquid cash resources, you tap into your non-liquid cash resource: retirement income that has been building in a retirement account. Through an ESOP, you're investing all or part of your money in the stock of your business instead of another company's stock.

The immediate gut reaction of some people is to resist this type of maneuver, and that reaction tends to be reinforced by financial advisors who would rather be responsible for managing your portfolio. Therefore, it's important to give you a little more information regarding this approach.

The first step is to think about how the financial advisor is managing your portfolio. To a great extent, they are investing your money in stocks, so you are basically taking an equity position with a number of companies, with the hope of a good return for your equity stake. That is what you are doing with your retirement funds today.

You are investing your retirement funds in the equity of businesses that are predominantly owned and controlled by other people, in hopes they do a good job in building the value of their business.

If that type of trust can be invested in "strangers," can it also be invested in yourself? If you have the confidence in your own ability to manage your company, that is the first obstacle to overcome.

So, how does this work? You start by forming a corporation. That corporation issues stock and sets up a retirement plan. Then, the corporation hires you. As a new employee, you roll all or part of your retirement funds into your new employer's retirement plan and then instruct the retirement plan to purchase stock in the corporation. At this point, the business is now funded with private equity and the stock in the business is legally owned by your retirement plan. Best of all, you are investing pre tax dollars—there are no taxes or withdrawal fees to pay.

Another way to think of this is to imagine you have been hired by Microsoft. Does Microsoft have a retirement plan? Yes, of course they do. When you become an employee, can you roll your retirement money into the Microsoft retirement program? Yes, of course you can. Is it possible that when you invest your money in stocks or mutual funds, you may end up owning stock in Microsoft? Yes, once again. This program is basically the same thing.

Once you have completed the transaction, you as an individual no longer own your business. Somebody in a better position owns the business: your retirement program owns the business. Why is that better? Because when the business makes money, you can choose to put money back into the retirement program, which is, of course, a tax deferred entity. Due to current ERISA law, you can set this retirement program up in such a way that you will be able to aggressively set money aside, and that's a nice benefit.

This program has been around for over a decade and is very well established, but it is not something you should try to set up at home or even with your local lawyer. ERISA law is complex and it is important to be an expert in this area of law to ensure the IRS is comfortable. There are organizations that specialize in this type of funding vehicle and they are listed in the resource section at www.educatedfranchisee. com.

▶ *Private equity investment*

Perhaps you know a venture capitalist, someone who looks for good business investment opportunities, but who does not want to be involved directly in the business. There are always folks looking to invest in a solid business opportunity and you may want to seek some of these folks out to find out what they would want in return for their funding. Often, a venture capitalist will command a majority ownership of the business, which may not be appealing to you but is worth learning about.

Just as there are brokers who can assist you in seeking loans, some brokers also specialize in finding equity investors.

GRANTS

Some people are under the impression there are grants commonly available as incentives for people to become entrepreneurs. Sometimes those impressions are created by strange television "pitch men" who would like to sell books that promise to connect you to these "miracle" funding sources.

You know the old saying, "If it sounds too good to be true ..." Well, you know the rest. According to Jim Parrish, finance counselor for the Florida Small Business Development Center at the University of South Florida, "Actually, fewer than one percent of new business startups benefit from government grants, and typically those are for businesses who focus on high-tech, biochemical and other forms of research." In all the years I have been involved with business startups, I have never known a person to secure a grant to start a business. Can it happen? Of course, anything could happen. Is likely to happen? No, it is not. This is the proverbial needle in a haystack approach and is usually the focus of people that are hoping to get something for nothing. Look in this area if you like but don't waste too much time here.

SUMMARY

As you begin to consider business investment, don't be victimized by "sticker shock." Investing in a business is comparable to investing in a home. Home buyers do not commonly pay cash—and neither do business buyers. Always remember that just as your investment in a home gives you an asset called "home," an investment in a business gives you an asset called "business."

In franchising, just as you'll find a wide variety of businesses and investment levels, you'll also find many types of financing. Business financing is an area where it pays to talk to specialists, not to just one person. Find out the pros and cons of the different types of financing discussed in this chapter and identify which makes the best sense for your particular situation.

Visit www.educatedfranchisee.com for a comprehensive list of reputable financing organizations.

Chapter 14

The Use Of Outside Experts

Many receive advice,
but the wise profit from it.
– Publilius Syrus

To date, most books on franchising fall into one of two common categories:

Cautionary advice from specific subject matter experts, such as lawyers, accountants, etc.

or

Inspirational stories of notable, even famous, entrepreneurs who "made it big."

In the first case, consultants with specific expertise try to impress upon you the urgency of hiring a fleet of highly trained experts to advise you on every step you take. They warn prospective franchise owners that they are prone to making costly mistakes and that success in a franchise business is jeopardized without meticulous review by experts.

On the other hand, the success stories of business pioneers, while motivational, are often devoid of advice about using consultants. They talk a lot more about their strategies and how they went about growing their businesses, and never mention the use of advisors at all.

The reality lies in the middle of these two extremes. There is significant value in the appropriate use of knowledgeable outside experts. The fact is, you need more than just inspiration to start a business. It's time to learn about how to appropriately use outside advice while making sure you maintain control of the process and the decision making.

The goal is to empower **you** to make independent decisions about the use of the various types of outside experts.

Most people do not need all the advisors some authors recommend. Depending on your background, there may be certain experts that are more necessary or useful than others.

Therefore, this chapter will describe the various types of advisors you may encounter and what you should expect from each of them:

- Franchise consultants

- Accountants

- Attorneys

- Financial and other advisors

But before we begin, I'd like to cover **five "Ground Rules of Outside Advice"** you should keep in mind as you consider the use of outside experts:

- **Ground Rule #1:** The role of any advisor is to give <u>advice</u>, and nothing more. It is not appropriate to delegate actual decisions to the advisors. It's your business, not theirs. So your job is to listen to their advice and then make your own decision based on the advice you receive.

- **Ground Rule #2:** You must check references and look at the experience of any advisor you are considering. It could be as simple as plugging their name or firm name into Yahoo or Google to see what results are returned. Just because they claim to be an advisor does not mean their advice is of value. Check their background.

- **Ground Rule #3:** The experience of the advisor should be relevant to the specific advice you are seeking. That may sound obvious, but it is surprising how often people will pose legal questions to their accountants. Each expert has their area of expertise. A franchise lawyer understands franchise law but may not be the best person to manage litigation and visa versa. Make sure you ask the right questions of the right person.

- **Ground Rule #4:** Consider the advisors' comments as they relate to their area of expertise and filter out opinions they may have about the specific business or industry. This is best accomplished by asking probing questions to determine how they formed their views. Remember, it is your job to learn about the business and their job to provide you with solid advice in their area of expertise.

- **Ground Rule #5:** An advisor should respect your decision. If you find an advisor is upset that you have elected not to follow a particular piece of advice, you should consider a change in advisors. Their job is to advise; your job is to decide.

If you follow these five ground rules in regard to dealing with outside advisors, you will be well on your way to determining which advisors will be important to you and which advisors you can do without. It will also assist you in making sure you remain in control of the due diligence process and remain the ultimate decision-maker.

TYPES OF CONSULTANTS/ADVISORS

The following is a list of the primary types of consultants and advisors you may consider using. The list is arranged in order of usage from the one you would probably use first to the one that would likely be used last.

▶ *Franchise consultant*

Sequentially, a franchise consultant is likely to be the first of the outside experts you will encounter in your research. In Chapter 9, we discussed how you would be likely to find a franchise consultant and begin a working relationship. We also discussed the fact that franchise consultants work in a similar capacity as executive recruiters and therefore should work free of charge to you. Here is how you can get the most from that relationship:

The goals of a good franchise consultant are to save you time, provide sound guidance and to give you a leg up with regard to targeting the companies with which you will perform due diligence.

Good franchise consultants are going to give you solid advice to make sure you're properly educated about the overall investigative process. They'll also have a group of outside advisors who can guide you in specific areas of expertise, including some that will be discussed in this chapter.

However, today there a lot of franchise consultant "wannabes" working the market. These are people with little or no experience who are looking at franchise consulting because they are afraid of going into franchises themselves. Or they already failed at another business endeavor and decided they'd rather just give advice.

Regrettably, this happens on a regular basis. Recently I worked with two men in separate cities who fit this description. Both were in the 55-60 age range. One of them had never owned a business and wanted to find something that he could run as a home-based business. The other had been involved in several so-called "business opportunities," but he had not achieved success with any of them.

Both men, after making a cursory review of several franchises, decided they would rather give franchise advice. Unfortunately, neither one of them had ever owned a franchise business nor had they worked for a franchisor, they had no previous knowledge of franchising. They were not even financially successful business people. How valuable do you think their advice would be?

So how do you find a great franchise consultant?

First, make sure you are working with a reputable company. Profile the company to make sure they have been in operation for more than five years, are members of the International Franchise Association and/or have more than 50 consultants in their system. You should also expect transparency. The website should provide a complete list of their consultants with respective background and expertise for each consultant.

Once you have identified a solid, proven franchise consulting company, you must make sure the franchise consultant has the skills and experience to help you. It is entirely appropriate to interview the franchise consultant and examine what type of track record they may have in or around franchising. Ask them for a biography. You must trust their experience, and their record of success.

If the franchise consultant is experienced and knowledgeable on franchising and business ownership, they can provide tremendous value to you and your search for the ideal business.

▶ Accountant to review P&L

Depending on your level of knowledge, the complexity of the business model and your overall comfort with the information you have gathered, you may want to employ an accountant to review the P&L you built in Chapter 13.

If you follow the approach described in Chapter 13, you will get the P&L line items and you will gain an understanding of how each line items works in that particular business. This is the basis of your P&L.

An accountant can be useful to validate whether you understand the P&L properly. If the accountant asks you some questions about the P&L that you can't answer, that can be an opportunity to return to the franchisees for clarification.

Keep in mind the prior caution about the accountant's expertise. They may raise questions that reflect they don't understand the particular business you're considering. Their job is to raise questions and your job is to conduct the due diligence process and get the questions answered. Please don't rely on an accountant to tell you if you will make money in a given business. Their crystal ball is no better than yours. The role of the accountant is to make sure you fully understand the numbers. You job is to determine if you can make the business work.

Don't surrender the decision-maker role. It's your most important job.

▶ Tax accounting

In my view, retaining the services of a good accountant on an ongoing basis is not an option—it's a MUST.

Every hour you spend in front of a computer trying to figure out the latest tax law interpretations or payroll issues is an hour that could have been spent on tasks much more relevant to driving business in the door.

It makes great sense to outsource bookkeeping, payroll processing and tax accounting to people who do it for a living. Your franchise consultant, franchisor or fellow franchisees are likely to have good recommendations of accountants who understand your business. Begin to build this relationship early in the process because every dollar you spend in the due diligence process, including the purchase of this book, may be a business expense and therefore can be paid for with pretax dollars.

▶ Franchise lawyer

The first word in this section title is important: *Franchise* lawyer. Lawyers have different areas of expertise. In this section we are discussing lawyers that specialize in franchise law.

As mentioned in the accounting section, the decision to use a franchise lawyer will depend on your level of knowledge, the complexity of the business model and your overall comfort with the information you have gathered. You may or may not want or need to use a lawyer to review the Franchise Disclosure Document and Franchise Agreement— that decision is yours to make.

As you'll recall from Chapter 7, the Franchise Disclosure Document is a document that is designed to be understood by the average person. You should not need a lawyer to read the information found in Items 1 - 23. By reading the Franchise Disclosure Document carefully, you should also be able to grasp the majority of the key aspects of the franchise relationship.

Despite your careful review of the Franchise Disclosure Document and the Franchise Agreement, there will be a number of areas that remain unclear. It is important for you to highlight all the passages in the franchise agreement that need explanation. In most cases, the franchisor will be ready with clear answers. If items remain confusing or you are simply looking for anther set of trained eyes to provide an unbiased review, then it is absolutely appropriate to consider a franchise attorney to review the document. About half of the people I work with end up using a franchise lawyer to review the franchise agreement and most spend between $1,000 and $3,000.

If you chose to have the franchise agreement reviewed by a trained franchise lawyer, please remember that most reputable franchises, particularly franchises of any significant size or maturity, have franchise agreements that are fundamentally non-negotiable. There may be instances where you are able to get a letter of clarification from the franchisor, but for the most part the franchise agreement is the same for everyone. This, of course, can be frustrating at times, but it is also the backbone of franchising. Uniformity of franchise agreements allows for equal treatment of all franchisees. If the franchisor regularly negotiates the franchise agreement, they will have a very difficult time holding everyone accountable to the same operational standards and maintaining consistency throughout the system.

As I mentioned, it makes good sense to give the Franchise Disclosure Document and franchise agreement a thorough study on your own as a first step to understanding the nature of the relationship. In the end, you will have to be comfortable living with the contract.

If you would like a list of attorneys that specialize in franchise law, go to the resource section of www.educatedfranchisee.com

▶ *Business lawyer*

The other type of legal advisor you'll need is a business lawyer. This attorney will help you set up your corporate entity for operating the business. The business lawyer will also help you structure your firm's by-laws and will provide you with your Articles of Incorporation.

While you may be able to conduct your own incorporation filing, it is best to minimize your liability by consulting with a business lawyer. In most cases this type of service should cost between $500 and $1,000.

▶ *Professional Employer Organization (PEO)*

Once you begin operations of your franchise, you may need to hire employees. Let's say you hire 10 employees—managing the paperwork surrounding those 10 employees can be challenging. Your responsibilities range from hiring/firing, training, retirement programs, workers compensation, payroll tax administration, etc. These are tasks that are not always the best use of your time. In order to simplify this, PEOs are becoming increasingly common in the franchise sector.

A PEO is an organization similar to an outsourced human resources department. As a matter of fact, YOU and your employees would actually become employees of the PEO. Your corporation would pay the PEO to conduct this service for you.

The PEO can help you save money, but more importantly, it can save you time, risk and headaches.

▶ *Retirement plan administrators*

You will recall from our earlier discussion of financing a business that many people use ESOPs as their funding source. Regardless of whether you use an ESOP to fund your business, you may want to consider a Defined Benefit Plan or a Profit Sharing Plan for your business. A retirement plan administrator can help you set up a retirement plan and manage it for the long term.

When you set up a retirement program, your business will make contributions to the fund within the parameters set up by the program. This approach allows you to aggressively save money that is tax deferred. There is a lot of detailed work that goes into this, and it is not advisable to manage this financial piece on your own.

▶ *Local real estate agents - after becoming a franchisee*

If location is important to your business, particularly if your franchise requires a prominent location, you are advised to consider working with a strong local real estate agent. This agent should be experienced working with franchise systems and willing to communicate with the franchisor's real estate department.

Your franchisor is not likely to know your market as well as you do, and you are not likely to know the market as well as a seasoned real estate professional. Keep in mind you should use a selection process in commercial real estate similar to the one you used in finding a good lawyer.

Take the time to get a few referrals and then interview the agents before making your choice. Also keep in mind that this service is normally free to you, since the landlord generally pays a commission to real estate agents for their work.

SUMMARY

As you consider the range of experts you may use in your franchise exploration process, please keep in mind:

DO NOT ABDICATE YOUR DECISION-MAKING RESPONSIBILITY!

Expert advisors are just that—advisors. They are not investing their money, time or emotion in the business, you are. Your chief duty as a franchise explorer is to synthesize all the information you collect and arrive at a well informed, fact-based decision that you personally feel good about.

If you get well qualified experts to perform duties in their areas of expertise that are relevant to your business, your prospects will be great for making a wise business decision.

Chapter 15

The Art Of Decision Making

*Every great leap forward in your life comes after
you have made a clear decision of some kind.*
– Brian Tracy

After all the information in this section, you may question the need for a chapter on decision-making.

At this point, it would seem to be as simple as deciding, "Yes, I want to do it" or "No, this isn't the right thing for me."

This is the hardest part for many people. Collecting information and assessing your skills and talents are activity-based tasks that don't demand commitment and therefore are comparatively easy. But choosing to take or avoid a specific course of action is a challenge. This is the time when you have to look in the mirror and say, "Yes, I can do this." That can be challenging.

"Will I be successful?" is the key concern people express when they are making a decision like this. The hard part is that we do not have a crystal ball so, to a certain extent, we have to take a leap of faith. That leap of faith is in two areas:

One, you have to believe in the business format. Second, you must believe in yourself enough to be willing to invest in yourself. All the due diligence you have conducted is done so you can make the very best decision possible. This chapter is about the moment of truth where you bring it all together to decide if this is the best course of action.

So how does the art of decision-making really work? Do you have an approach you use when it is time to make a decision? The answer is usually "Yes." Over the years, we have all developed approaches to decision making. These approaches generally fall into one of two categories:

1) One category could be described as logical or left-brained. You take the information, your calculator, and at the same time start grading the alternatives. These are the folks who often say, "It is all about the numbers, nothing else matters to me."

2) The other type of decision maker is the intuitive or right-brained person. This type of decision maker has to "feel right" about the business. They trust their gut and figure everything else will work itself out. Most of these folks say to me, "I really need to like the business and be passionate about it."

Are you the more logical, analytical type? Or are you the intuitive, right-brain type? Whichever the case may be, two common tendencies are:

- To lean toward the style we find most comfortable.

- To recognize we probably should acknowledge and use our "opposite" side for balance in our decision-making.

One of the biggest mistakes we make in decision making is refusing to acknowledge that this type of decision must be right on BOTH sides of our brain. If you are logical, you must also "feel" right about the step you are taking. If you are more intuitive, you must also use a logical approach to make sure you don't move into a business in which you will not be happy.

My methodology to decision making uses both approaches in order to make sure you have a great chance of making the correct decision. I cannot tell you what the correct decision is, but I can tell you that if you focus on making sure you are comfortable on all levels, you will be well positioned for success.

THE LOGICAL APPROACH

The logical approach really has to be the first priority regardless of your natural tendency. Intuitive decision making works best when you have a good handle on the factual information. At this point in the process, you have spent a considerable amount of time in the information gathering stage. This is the time to pull all of the information together into a factual, logical structure.

I am going to provide two examples of structures you may want to use as you create a logical decision making matrix. The examples I will provide are simply that—examples. If you feel you would like to improvise, add to or change the structure, please feel free to do so. Just make sure the decision making matrix is logical and reflective of the information you have gathered.

▶ Ranking Methodology

Step 1 - Brainstorm all the things that are important to you in a business. Go back to the work you did in Chapter 3 and other chapters in which you considered the relevant factors for business entry and business success. What is important to you? What does your box look like? Make a master list of all the factors. There is no need to prioritize it yet, and it doesn't matter if the list is long. Just make sure all the factors are listed, no matter how seemingly insignificant.

Step 2 - Narrow the master list down to a maximum of 10 criteria. As you whittle the list, make sure the list is reflective of your needs and desires. Don't include an item just because someone else said it should be important. Only include those items that are honestly important to you. In the end, this will be your business if you choose to move forward. If it truly is important to you to "never work on weekends again," then list it.

Step 3 - It's time to construct a matrix for grading and comparing the companies you are investigating. Grade each company on each criterion you have listed. Try to be as honest as possible. If you don't remember, go back to your notes, and if you cannot find the information, make some more calls. You need to be able to answer each question for each company correctly and factually. I would suggest you award points based on the following system:

- + 2 points for being an outstanding match

- + 1 point for matching your need

- 0 points for a neutral ranking

- − 1 point for not matching your need

- − 2 points for being in conflict with your need

Assess the companies separately, as opposed to grading each of your top 10 variables for all the companies. Hopefully you'll avoid a tendency to skew the rankings with intuition by ranking the companies side-by-side. That's a comparison you'll make as you tally the results.

Step 4 - When you've graded the companies in each of the categories, then it's time to add/subtract points for each of the companies and arrive at their final scores.

I have an example of this approach for three companies below:

Example of ranking technique:

	Ranking		
	Company A	Company B	Company C
Speed of break even	-2	0	2
Monday - Friday	-1	2	2
Predictability	0	2	0
Quality of support	2	2	2
Resale vaulation	0	1	1
Investment < 150K	-1	2	1
Enjoyable	2	1	1
Employee management	0	-1	1
Strong marketing program	-2	-2	-1
Cash on cash return	0	0	-1
Total points	**-2**	**7**	**8**

Company A   – 2 points (Unacceptable)

Company B   + 7 points (Acceptable)

Company C   + 8 points (The best)

Using a ranking approach, it is clear Company A is not a good match. It is also clear Company C is the best match but is closely followed by Company B.

▶ Ranking and Weighting Approach

Another way to logically sort the information on the companies is to include both ranking and weighting in the table. For those who may not be familiar with this type of approach, what you are doing is allowing for the fact that some of the criteria may be more important than other criteria. By ranking the companies and weighting the criteria, you may end up with a more accurate representation. This is especially important if several of the characteristics are significantly more important than other criterion.

Steps 1 and 2 are the same as above.

<u>Step 3</u> – Allocate 100 points among the ten (or fewer) criteria. For example, if you have 10 criteria and one is of average importance, it should receive 10 points. If one is twice as important as the average, give that criterion 20 points and so on.

<u>Step 4</u> – Rank each company on each criterion using the same technique as above.

+ 2 points for being an outstanding match

+ 1 point for matching your need

  0 points for a neutral ranking

– 1 point for not matching your need

– 2 points for being in conflict with your need

<u>Step 5</u> – Multiply the ranking by the weight and then sum the totals for each company. Please see the example below:

Example of Weighting and Ranking Technique:

		Company A		Company B		Company C	
	Weight	Ranking	Total	Ranking	Total	Ranking	Total
Criteria 1	Speed of break even	8	-2	-16	0	0	2	16
Criteria 2	Monday - Friday	12	-1	-12	2	24	2	24
Criteria 3	Predictability	15	0	0	2	30	0	0
Criteria 4	Quality of support	4	2	8	2	8	2	8
Criteria 5	Reaale valuation	12	0	0	1	12	1	12
Criteria 6	Investment < 150K	17	-1	-17	2	34	1	17
Criteria 7	Enjoyable	5	2	10	1	5	1	5
Criteria 8	Employee management	8	0	0	-1	-8	-1	-8
Criteria 9	Strong marketing program	5	-2	-10	-2	-10	-1	-5
Criteria 10	Cash on cash return	14	0	0	0	0	1	14
	Total Points	100		-37		95		83

- Company A – -37 points (Unacceptable)
- Company B – 95 points (The best)
- Company C – 83 points (Acceptable)

As you can see, by weighting the criteria, we now see that Company B is actually the best pure match to our needs and desires. Without the weighting, we may not have known this.

With many ways to conduct this type of analysis, feel free to be "logically creative." Just make sure you take into account each of the areas that are truly important to you and be sure to honestly appraise each company in regard to the criteria. Now it's time to move on to the all-important gut-level impressions.

THE INTUITIVE APPROACH

Once you have completed the logical approach, gather up all your work and put it away! Seal it in an envelope. It isn't that you want to discard the information, but now you'll want to take the information that's fresh in your mind and put it to use on the intuitive side.

Go to your special spot. We all have it—it's that special place where we do our best thinking. For some of us, it's while we're driving, or it could be a quiet place where you typically do your most productive work, or it could be in the hot tub.

When you get to that special spot, make sure you don't have any distractions or time constraints.

Relax, close your eyes and envision yourself in five years being an owner in Company A. With your vision of your future in your head, ask yourself these questions:

- How am I spending my day?
- Am I enjoying what I am doing?
- Who is around me?
- Am I happy?
- Have I created a life based on what is important to me?

- How much freedom and control am I experiencing?

- How successful am I?

- Have I created wealth?

- Am I feeling energized and motivated?

Spend some time connecting and playing with this future. Make the vision as clear as you can. How does it feel?

Every great athlete uses visualization techniques. Every great leader uses visualization techniques. In this case, you are using it as a tool to tap into your "right brain." As you envision your future with Company A, how is your body responding? Pay attention to your physiological response. Are you stressed? Are you relaxed? Are you energized?

Once this feels real and you have called upon your gut, go through this same process with Company B and C. If you're contemplating staying in or returning to traditional employment, it's a good idea to go through this envisioning exercise, too, for that scenario.

I would advise against bringing your friends, family, pastor or anyone else into this process. Hopefully you have spoken to them on this subject and know how they feel. What is most important to remember during the process is that this is your decision.

Dig deep inside yourself and listen to your GUT. In the vast majority of cases, one company will "feel" best to you.

BRINGING THE APPROACHES TOGETHER

Now it is time to determine which business is the best fit for you. It is time to marry the two approaches. There are a limited number of possible outcomes, so I would like to go through each possible outcome and share with you some thoughts.

Outcome #1 – Your logical and intuitive feelings are the same. This is ideal and easy. You chose the company that passed all the tests.

Outcome #2 – You have a strong favorite on one side and not on the other side. If your gut is screaming Company B but your analytical side says Company C is slightly better, go with the stronger feeling: Company

B. If the logical approach clearly prefers Company C but your intuitive approach is only slightly in favor of Company B, go with Company C.

Outcome #3 – Your logical and intuitive sides are opposite. Logic says Company C is the best and Company A is clearly mismatched to your goals and objectives. At the same time your intuitive approach says you can see yourself owning Company A and not Company C. This is a time to be very careful. Earlier we discussed a sales person that bought a retail golf store because he loved golf. The company ended in failure because the business did not give him the things he really needed to be happy. This may be an indication you should stop and reevaluate.

FEAR IN DECISION MAKING

Remember our earlier discussion of fear in Chapter One. Making a decision like this never means your confidence is so high that you are completely free of fear. Quite the opposite! This is the time when you will normally experience the highest level of fear. If you didn't, that would be unusual.

In Chapter One we discussed fear in some depth. Remember that fear, mixed with the human psyche, results in one of two reactions: motivation or paralysis.

Seventy percent of successful business people report they are primarily motivated by the fear of failure. The other thirty percent report they are mostly motivated by the need for success. It is clear that fear of failure is a powerful emotion and can be a great asset in the drive toward success—if you are able to harness it.

Paralysis can have the opposite effect. If you find you are paralyzed and cannot seem to make a decision either way, please be careful about owning a business. Business is about making timely decisions every day. You need to be able to do this in order to be successful. If you are too scared to make a decision, you will not make the decisions that are required as a business owner and risk failure. Look at yourself in the mirror and ask yourself if you can harness the power of fear to spur you forward and create success. Remember these words:

> *Courage is resistance to fear, mastery*
> *of fear – not absence of fear.*
> – Mark Twain

SUMMARY

The exercise in this chapter is just one of many alternatives you can use in shaping a great business decision. Of course, both general approaches, logical and intuitive, are sound and valuable. You may have developed or utilized some tools for decision-making that have worked really well for you, but if you don't have proven methods readily at hand, give these a try.

Don't forget that the primary goal is to MAKE A DECISION! Your willingness to follow the vision and to decisively move toward your goals is one of the most critical success factors for an entrepreneur, a true leader. This is probably the first test of whether you have the characteristics to be a future business owner.

Part III

**YOU'VE FOUND THE RIGHT BUSINESS:
NOW THE JOURNEY BEGINS**

Introduction

Maximize certainty and minimize risk. That's the success formula everyone would like to employ, whether it's in a business context or in their personal life.

And regardless of your background, you know that 100% certainty, while something to strive for, is impossible. It seems there is always something that can trip you up along the way, no matter how well prepared you are.

The trick is to smooth out the peaks and valleys that are inevitable in business or in any aspect of life.

Reducing the number and depth of the valleys is a high priority for nearly all of us. Part III is designed to do just that, to help you avoid some of the pitfalls of business entry and to help you understand and cope with the setbacks you can't avoid.

The following examination of the stages of franchisee development will show you what to expect, but it doesn't necessarily advise you to sidestep any particular stage. Instead, this metaphor of life's progression from infancy to elder adulthood explains how and why each stage is not only inevitable but also quite useful in the growth of your business.

At one time or another, most of us have thought, "If I only knew then what I know now..." It may be true that we'd love to apply our experience retroactively, but how many of us would truly like to have skipped the formative years of our youth?

The advantage of this section is to apply the advantage of foresight to the stages of development and be able to anticipate many of the "speed bumps" on the road ahead.

In addition, Part III shares advice to help you successfully navigate through the various stages of your own development and the evolution of your business.

What is your mindset as you leave the starting gate? And what will it be as you pass through the stages of development? Those are questions that you'll want to address before and during your journey.

And now is the time to determine how to benchmark your progress and measure your success. After all, if you're not keeping score, how do you know you're winning?

And finally, I'll look at the ultimate step that should be considered before you take any of the others—your exit strategy, the selling of your business.

It may be difficult to ask you to focus on selling your business when you're still excited about your prospects for entering and growing a business! But if the finish line isn't in sight, or at least in mind, it will be difficult to know how to benchmark your success.

Chapter 16

The Steps Of Franchise Development

Coming together is a beginning, staying together
is progress, and working together is success.
— Henry Ford

Picture this: You've completed a thorough self-examination; you've answered the tough questions about whether you're ready to be an entrepreneur; you've studied franchises and narrowed them down to the one that's just right for you; you've gotten good advice from the right experts, and you've taken the plunge into franchise business ownership.

So what's the first thing you do as a new franchisee? **You forget what you bought!**

You probably expected the answer to be something like plan a grand opening, or print my business cards, or join the Chamber of Commerce. And those are all good things for the new business owner to undertake.

Unfortunately, forgetting what you bought is a common occurrence for new owners.

Why does that happen? Considering all the preparation that leads up to a franchise purchase, how could new owners possibly forget what they bought?

After the contract is signed, the first inclination of many new owners is to ask themselves a series of questions such as, "What do I do next? What kind of marketing tactic should I try? What type of office do I need?" They often forget that what they bought was the right to use the franchisor's operating system. The operating system should be designed to answer every one of your questions in an organized, efficient manner.

Consequently, the first step you, as a new business owner, should take is not really an action at all. Instead, what I advise is to take a moment and review the operating system you just purchased. Contact the franchisor and say, "I have a few questions. Who is my contact person for support services and how do we get the ball rolling?" From that point forward, you need to rely on your support person to efficiently guide you toward the opening of your business and beyond.

During your due diligence you studied the quality of the franchise operating system. You then signed a franchise agreement giving you the right to use the operating system. Make sure you fully rely on the operating system from the first day.

THE STAGES OF FRANCHISEE MATURITY

Most people entering a franchise system for the first time are unaware of the natural maturation process they will go through. They do not fully appreciate the nature of the relationship and the various ways in which a person can give and receive value within the franchise community.

To more fully explain this process, I will first discuss "The Five Stages of Franchisee Development" using the analogy of personal growth and development for illustration and the typical timing for each of the stages. After discussing the five stages, I will delve into the driving forces behind these stages.

▶ Stage 1: Infancy

In the life cycle of a franchisee, this is the phase from contract signing to the opening of the business. This is also the "I forgot what I bought" stage, where you're being "spoon fed" by the franchisor, and frankly, that is something you probably need.

You know nothing about this new world and the franchisor support staff is talking with you almost daily, making sure you're getting your questions answered and all your needs met. They're really teaching you how to walk, and in most cases franchisees don't take a step without consulting the franchisor.

A high quality franchisor is maintaining this almost constant contact for two great reasons:

For one, it is in the franchisor's best interests, as well as yours, to make sure you are groomed for both a quick start and long-term success. Any good franchisor knows that system strength and growth are contingent upon successful franchisees.

The second reason is that many people encounter some uncertainty after they sign the franchise agreement and before they open for operations. In marketing courses this is commonly called *post purchase dissonance*. Any wrong step you take may have a significantly negative effect on your confidence level. A high quality franchisor will be there with you during this initial stage to make sure you are comfortable and confident and that you successfully lay the foundation of your business.

At this stage, allow yourself to lean on the franchisor. You have just given them a tidy sum of money and you should take advantage of the fact that nothing is expected of you other than following the step-by-step guidelines to open the business. Enjoy this stage, as it is wonderful and exciting to be part of something new.

▶ Stage 2: Childhood

Franchisee childhood starts with the opening of the business and typically lasts through the first six to 12 months of operation. In this phase, you're learning and growing just as children do through their formative years. You're bombarded with lots of information, and at times it's all you can do to keep your head above water.

At this stage, you are likely to enjoy a strong relationship with the franchisor, much like the bond between young students and their favorite teachers or advisors. You're learning the ABC's of the business and eventually learning to problem solve on your own, using what you've learned.

In this stage, the value proposition for the franchisee is typically very high because the franchisor is focusing considerable time and energy on the franchisee's education. At the same time, the royalty payments are relatively low. That combination tends to create a strong sense of value.

To extend our school metaphor, franchisees are graduating from the ABC's to writing essays, so everyone is excited about the progress.

Since the franchisor is vastly more knowledgeable than the franchisee, the operating system is generally followed quite closely.

▶ *Stage 3: Adolescence*

Naturally, the turmoil that can accompany the "adolescent years" needs no explanation. Even if you haven't raised a teenager, you've certainly been one! At this stage in the life of a franchise, the "teen years" extend from perhaps the second year in business for a year or two. And it's a phase that really tests the relationship between franchisor and franchisee.

In this stage, franchisees may not be learning as much. They aren't listening as much, and there is also less to learn. The foundational knowledge about the franchise has already been learned, and it may be that franchisees are a bit tired of the repetition.

Franchisees may have a tendency to rebel at this point and think they may have a better way of doing things and would like to test themselves. As clichéd as it sounds, it is common at this stage for the franchisee to feel the franchisor "just does not understand" their situation.

Another thing to remember is that the Law of Diminishing Returns has set in at this point. Royalty payments have increased as your business becomes more successful, but the amount of incremental learning delivered from the franchisor is decreasing. This can contribute to the desire for independence.

Strain in the relationship is quite common and something that should be anticipated by both franchisor and franchisee.

▶ *Stage 4: Adulthood and Parenthood*

After the franchisee has passed through the turbulent adolescent years, they begin to feel more a part of the family. This family includes both the franchisor and the franchisees. Franchisees begin to recognize the mutual strengths and weaknesses of all members of the franchise system.

The more experienced franchisee begins to see the value of being part of a solid system, acting in a mentoring role for others who have joined. The franchisees are willing to listen more to the franchisor, as they see the common bond of working to strengthen the overall system. Recruiting and supporting new franchisees becomes a much higher priority, with peer-to-peer relationships being valued more highly.

As the franchisee moves into the "Adult/Parent" stage, they often begin to realize there is significant value in the collective knowledge of the entire franchise system. Whereas a franchisee in "adolescent" stage may call franchisees to complain, the "Adult" franchisee tends to spend more time on the phone with other franchisees sharing ideas and ways to use the franchise operating system more effectively. Learning to lead within a franchise system takes maturity, and it can be tremendously satisfying both personally and financially—especially when you are part of the growth that helps to shape a company into an industry leader.

▶ *Stage 5: Elder Statesman*

When you've been in a franchise business for five years, you typically enjoy an "elder statesman" role in the organization. You become someone who is regarded as one of the "pillars of the system," a franchisee that others want to speak with and learn from at company conferences.

Chances are you will have mentored a number of other franchisees who have come into the system more recently. And the franchisor values you highly because you tend to be a strong supporter and promoter of the system.

At this stage, the franchisor will often call you to ask your advice on subjects facing the system and try to get your point of view on various potential solutions. The franchisor may also ask you to take on projects for the overall improvement of the system. In many ways you become a trusted bridge between the franchisor and the franchisee community.

WHY DO WE GO THROUGH THESE STAGES?

If you are like me, the fact that there are stages of development is interesting, but I always want to know *why*. If I know why, then it is often easier for me to understand my own thinking and to adjust accordingly. As you look at "The Five Stages of Franchisee Maturity," there are a number of ways to explain the natural maturing process. A psychologist would approach the analysis differently than a sociologist. My experience tells me it is a mixture of approaches that tends to work best.

Most new franchisees don't fully understand the value proposition during the initial stages of development and they don't fully appreciate the fact that the franchisor needs to be able to make a profit in order to survive and prosper. New franchisees also seem to underestimate the value of being a part of a strong, healthy franchise system in which the franchisor and their fellow franchisees are all successful.

Let's focus on just the franchisor value proposition and how it relates to royalty payments. This will give you a basic understanding of value

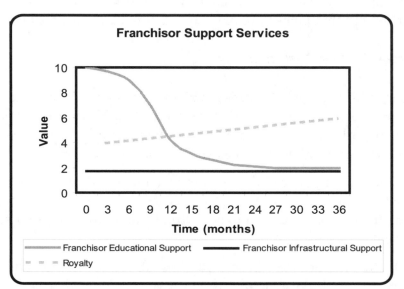

As you can see by the previous graphic, in the early stages of the franchise relationship the franchisee is gaining tremendous value for the royalty investment. The franchisor is delivering both structural and educational support services, the value of which far exceed the cost of the royalty. As a result, the franchisee is generally satisfied with the relationship.

It is also important to note that in the first year of operations, it is normal for a franchisor to lose money on that individual franchisee. The franchisor is investing for the long-term success and potential royalty stream.

Somewhere around the 12-month mark, the royalty and support services lines cross. By this time, you have learned much of what you need to know to run your business successfully. Although the franchisor is still able to provide educational support to some degree, the learning curve is beginning to flatten. Most of the support is infrastructure-related support, such as marketing, purchasing, software and so on. The total value of the support services declines while your royalty often will go up. The franchisor is finally able to make profit off you and you now begin to believe that you know most of what you need to know to run your business. This is the driver behind Stage 3: Adolescence.

So, what drives us beyond this point? How do we mature past our teenage years and once again find value in the franchise system? The driver is we finally begin to appreciate the overall value of the entire system. This includes the value of having fellow franchisees that often become close personal friends and can be exceptionally supportive.

You also begin to understand that the franchisor is human, and that the franchisor's profit is what fosters reinvestment and growth, which builds the future for everyone. In other words, to paraphrase a well-known saying, you finally stop asking, "What can my franchise system do for me?" and begin asking, "What can I do for my franchise system?" with the full understanding that a strong franchise system pays dividends to you and your business.

Here is a graphic illustration of that set of circumstances:

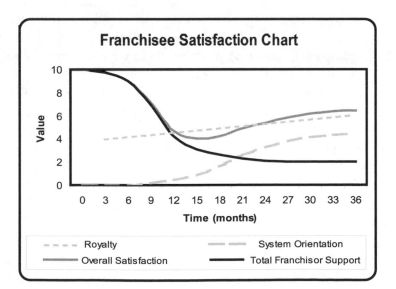

This illustration is nearly the same as the previous graph. The only difference is that I have added an additional line that representing the overall System Orientation of the franchisee, and I have added a line representing Overall Satisfaction. The Overall Satisfaction line is the cumulative result of the Franchisor Support and the System Orientation lines.

As you follow the Overall Satisfaction line, you see there is a period of time where the line dips below the Royalty Line. After that, due to the effect of the franchisee's increase in System Orientation, Overall Satisfaction once again surpasses Royalty and satisfaction is regained.

SUMMARY

Knowing about these "life stages" does not mean you can, or should, avoid any of them. You wouldn't typically advise a youngster to skip any of the natural phases of life, and the same goes for the business life cycle.

These are phases that are pretty consistent throughout franchising, and frankly, it is more important to understand the ups and downs than it is to sidestep them. Try to improve your understanding and set expectations more realistically. Awareness will, in most cases, help you get through some agonizing times as you encounter challenges in your business.

In particular, be aware of the Law of Diminishing Returns and the impact it can have on your relationship with the franchisor. The value proposition changes as you mature in your understanding of the relationship and become more comfortable. Remember, your long-term business relationship affords you the opportunity to build strong, meaningful personal relationships. Over time you will work with both key members of the franchisor's staff and your fellow franchisees to grow your business and your life.

Chapter 17

Key Items For Success In A Franchise System

Life is a succession of lessons which
must be lived to be understood.
– Ralph Waldo Emerson

As you enter business ownership, there are four areas of advice that can be critical for your success. Sometimes people have a tendency to "over-think" the situation, when the better approach would be to focus on a few of the critical success factors.

That's not to say you should ignore detailed analysis. I'm not discounting the value of carefully examining all of the factors that contribute to your business decision. In fact, reasoned analysis is essential, not optional.

But to position yourself for success as a franchisee, you should focus on these key concepts as your guideposts.

Remember that becoming a franchisee is not the destination, it is the starting line. And now, after you've become a franchisee, you have to perform. So in this chapter, I'll discuss concepts you may have heard before, but they bear repeating. I've prioritized and condensed what I feel are the most important.

I recommend you focus on these factors:

•   Leverage positive thinking

•   Eliminate entitlement thinking

•   Make a two-year commitment

•   Set your top three measurable productivity goals.

Let me discuss each of these and why they are so important.

LEVERAGE POSITIVE THINKING

Many great books have been written on the power of positive thinking, and many of us have favorite authors and lecturers in this category. I certainly am one of the believers. I know what a huge difference positive thinking can make in a business. I appreciate and utilize that power in my own business every day.

If you believe something will happen, there is a significantly better chance that it actually will happen. Ask any athletic coach about how they prepare players for victory, and the response will be consistent; you MUST put positive thoughts in the forefront as you head into a competition if you want to have any hope of winning.

The coach doesn't gather the players around him and say, "Team, I know there are a lot of things that can go wrong out there today and hopefully we'll avoid them!" That's not exactly an invigorating thought to take with you to the playing field.

Instead, the coach of even the underdog squad will describe the impending contest this way, "When we execute our game plan and do everything we've worked on in practice, we'll come out on top."

In reality, a certain amount of positive energy is available to us each day. It is your duty to engage and direct as much of your positive energy as you can, so a key first step is to make sure you're spending time in positive situations.

Now I know that sounds fairly elementary, a case of "easier said than done." But you can employ strategies that will stack the deck in your favor as you approach the various situations you will confront each business day.

We all know of three types of situations awaiting us every day:

1) Good situations, the ones that give us pleasure

2) Neutral situations, inconsequential occurrences that pass without much notice

3) Negative situations, the road blocks that impede our success

Fortunately, life is typically filled with mostly good and neutral situations, with the bulk of them being the neutral, routine day-to-day events and actions. The key to managing and maintaining a strong supply of positive energy is to minimize the number and impact of negative situations.

▶ Visioning

To protect your positive energy, begin your day with visioning exercises that focus your thinking on positive outcomes for the day. Any successful business leader will testify about the power of actually posting visual representations of your goals and reciting goals out loud. Again, if you think good things are going to happen, there is a better chance they will.

As awkward as it may seem initially, it really helps to post visioning statements at your work station and recite them every day—aloud. Hearing your vision statements in the open air adds real meaning and impact to them, impressions that you'll carry into your business day.

▶ Solve Negatives Quickly

Another behavior that can make a huge difference for you is to solve negatives quickly and make sure you do not dwell on them. A disruption of positive energy can really throw you off track, as evidenced so often in athletics. The greatest coaches emphasize the important of "being in the present." Athletes are coached to have very short memories when it comes to making a costly error.

I once had a client who was ideally suited in many respects for a particular franchise he was exploring. But as he was preparing for his due diligence, he was victimized by credit card fraud, as someone in another city charged $2,000 worth of goods to his account. Obviously identity theft is a serious matter and warrants urgent attention. But in this man's case, the issue consumed him.

I kept in touch with him over the course of nine months. During that time he became so engulfed in trying to resolve every detail and in seeking retribution that he not only lost track of franchise exploration, but he also lost his job. So what started as a $2,000 financial hardship escalated to something much more costly in many ways.

It was all because he could not limit the amount of time that he focused on the negative situation.

Without exception, we all experience setbacks. Again, the trick is to limit the time we spend in those negative situations and to move on to the next opportunity as quickly as possible.

▶ *Watch the company you keep*

Want to be a successful business person? Then hang around successful business people! In all walks of life, we choose our surroundings, whether in social or business circles. So as you identify people you want to spend time with, why not make a point of targeting positive, successful people?

This concept is particularly important in a franchise setting. By associating with franchisees that are proven leaders, you have two major things to gain from them:

The first is knowledge. Lifelong learning is critical to your achievement level in franchising, so it only makes sense to learn from all the lessons a veteran franchisee can share. Believe me; they'll have as much to share with you about their failures as they do about their triumphs.

But even more important than knowledge is the vast amount of positive energy you can absorb from these business leaders. Whether in conference calls or company meetings, the standout performers typically have the ability to inspire through their words of encouragement. Keep in mind they have dual purposes for motivating you. One, of course, is altruistic. They simply care about people and want to see them do well. Another business reason is that they want to see you succeed. Your success, and that of other new franchisees, helps raise the level of the overall franchise, thereby boosting the value of the business.

Keep in mind, however, that associating with like-minded leaders is a two-way street. You should plan to give positive energy back to the group, not just drain energy from it. Ask yourself, "Why would the leaders want me to be around them? What value can I contribute?"

After all, successful franchisees will avoid "desperation call" situations that will take energy away from them. They know that "like attracts like," so they hope to surround themselves with people who bring some positive energy with them.

The bottom line is that if you spend your time hanging around with dissatisfied, negative-thinking people, your outlook gets clouded. Choose to live in a positive mental environment and protect your right to live there.

ELIMINATE ENTITLEMENT THINKING

Entitlement thinking may be the most hazardous pitfall for franchisees. It's a way of thinking that is all too often bred in corporate America, where employees find themselves feeling, and saying, the company owes them more. If you have a corporate background, how often have you observed or experienced bitterness due to a downsizing or a bonus that "should have been bigger"?

Unfortunately, entitlement thinking extends too many aspects of everyday life, as evidenced by the litigious nature of our society. Consider the many lawsuits filed because people need to blame someone else for their problems. A friend who owned a storefront business was sued because someone stumbled on the curb outside his restaurant. This person then claimed the curb was one inch higher than regulations permitted at the point where they tripped! In the end the insurance company paid this individual because they tripped.

What an example of entitlement thinking! This person believed someone owed them something instead of asking if they could have done something to avoid tripping, like lifting their foot one inch higher. A person taking full responsibility for their actions would have said, "Darn, I scraped my knee. I should have watched where I was going." Today we see a tremendous gap in personal responsibility.

A successful business owner does not blame others. They look in the mirror and say, "What can I do to fix this situation?" As you'll recall from the previous chapter on the stages of franchisee development, there can be a tendency at times to blame the franchisor if things aren't going as planned. A business owner cannot afford to engage in disempowering thinking and behavior.

To achieve success in a franchise business, you have to embrace full accountability. Buying a franchise does not mean the franchisor will make your business a success. They'll help you, of course, but they won't do your work for you.

If sales performance in your business does not measure up to your expectations in your new business, you must step up and be responsible for your own success. Sure, you could indulge in self-pity, but what purpose would it serve? If the franchise you bought is based on a proven model and others are experiencing success, then you need to challenge yourself to correct the course.

Think about the regal lion we admire at the zoo. In captivity, the lion is accustomed to being fed regularly every day. But if that lion was released in the Serengeti, how much time do you think he'd be able to spend thinking about the unfairness of not being fed by the zookeeper? You find very little entitlement thinking in the Serengeti!

MAKE A TWO-YEAR COMMITMENT

As you contemplate investment in a franchise business, do NOT make the mistake of equating the expression "proven model" with "instant success." Many franchises do not make earnings claims at all, and those that do make no guarantees about immediate cash flow.

You should build a solid business plan and then stick to it for at least a two-year period. The first year of business is, to a great extent, laying the foundation for future success. In the second year, you build upon that foundation, and that's when you should make a serious evaluation of your performance.

One franchisor related a story about three new franchisees who entered their sales and training process at the same time. One of the prospects quit before completing the formal training and returned to the work world. A second prospect became discouraged after a few months and eventually sold the business. The third new franchisee finished in the bottom quartile after the first year in business. Not deterred, the franchisee kept his head down and focused on the business plan. The next year that same franchisee finished #1 in sales performance. The franchisee followed their business plan by laying a strong foundation during the first year and then building on that foundation in the second year.

In most cases, particularly with those who are new to franchising, developing new skill sets takes time and patience. The first months in business are rarely accurate predictors of long-term success. Instead, it is wise to measure yourself against your business plan in three-month increments for the first year and for a while thereafter.

It is critical to be honest in your self-appraisals. The biggest reason for failing is not undercapitalization; it is a lack of commitment. It's an unwillingness to give the business at least a two-year effort.

Remember, the first year is foundation building; the second year is business building. A two-year commitment is the only way to be fair to both yourself and your business.

SET YOUR TOP THREE PRODUCTIVITY MEASURES

You've read dozens of articles and books, heard dozens of lectures about the importance of goal-setting. So you certainly don't need another book *preaching* to you about goals.

Nevertheless, I'll take a risk and add a different dimension to the goal-setting dialogue. It is probably clear to you already that you cannot expect to achieve great things unless you know what those great things that you're trying to achieve are.

To put it another way, how do you know you've arrived if you don't know where you're going?

Your goals aren't real until you write them down and truly buy into them. But just setting goals is not enough, the process is not complete.

I urge you to set your top three productivity measures for your new franchise business, post them prominently, and monitor them regularly.

Let me make the important distinction between productivity measures and goals. It is important, even vital, to have goals, but those goals are often expressed as a fixed number or a "finish line." I value productivity measures because you can, and should, use them all the time. Productivity measures are the indicators that tell you if you're making progress toward your goals—that's where I see the value.

Why the top three? Because if you list too many measures, you can get bogged down in the minutia of specific tactics that are needed for each of them. You should devote most of your energy and effort toward the most important things you want to achieve and not be distracted from them. If you've set too many goals and measures, you may have a tendency to pick the low-hanging fruit, just for the sake of checking off items from your "to do" list.

When you have your top three productivity measures committed to paper, then it's time to inject serious discipline into your time management. Make sure that every task you're doing is focused on these three criteria. Ask yourself:

"Is what I'm doing right now positively impacting one of my productivity measures?

What else could I be doing that would have a positive impact on my productivity measures? Can the value of what I'm doing right now be checked by one of my productivity measures?"

If not, stop doing it now! Does that mean you should never do it? No. It just means you shouldn't be doing it during hours when your most important top three productivity measures must be pursued and your progress accurately measured. A good example is paying bills. Is that essential? Of course it is. But is it essential to do it during optimum marketing and sales time? That's an easy one to answer.

Ironically, one of the benefits of prominently displaying and always pursuing your top three productivity measures is that you can change them when it's necessary. That may sound contradictory to my earlier statement about "stick-to-it-ness," but the goals and measures that don't change are the ones left on a shelf and largely ignored. Your productivity measures will change as your business matures and your expertise grows.

Amending your top three productivity measures from time to time is a positive, refreshing experience. It means you're keeping close watch on your progress, and learning a lot from your successes and failures. And that's a sign of positive business growth.

SUMMARY

You'll note that two of the critical success factors in this chapter are all about "being" and "doing." They go hand-in-hand, and neither of them does well without the other.

Your mindset has to be positive and forward-thinking to achieve success as a franchisee. Do everything you can do to stack the deck in your favor in terms of positive thinking, positive situations and positive people. By the way—it helps quite a lot if you are a positive person yourself!

Go into your business with a great attitude about self-accountability, rather than waiting for someone else to wave a magic wand that will make your problems disappear.

Those are the factors that relate to getting your "head space" adjusted properly, but all the positive thinking in the world is pretty much useless without concrete action backing it up. This is why a solid, long-term commitment and a challenging, published goal set of goals and measures are vital ingredients, too.

Chapter 18

Conclusion

*Twenty years from now you will be more disappointed in
the things that you didn't do than in the ones you did do.*
– Mark Twain

Success is all about creating your own future. A simple reality to
remember is: Those who are not working for their own dream are
working for someone else's dream.

We have all held jobs and conducted work that has enriched
someone else. It is time for you to create your own vision, to build your
own box. This process will take some time and you may need to enlist
the help of a friend or a franchise consultant, but don't shortcut the
process. By conducting the upfront work properly and making sure you
know what you want, you will be much more effective in determining if
the opportunity is right for you.

Next, be dogged about finding the right opportunity that fits your
box. Be friendly, engaging, curious and focused in exploring opportunities.
Whatever you do, don't get discouraged; the right opportunity does
exist—you simply need the patience to find it. By using the right tools,
you will be able to fully answer every question about the business
opportunity prior to making a final decision. Use the tools and make
the right decision.

Once you have chosen the right business, understand that it will
take time and focus to build your dream business. Remember, successful
business owners are not the smartest, brightest or luckiest. They did
not wait for the perfect time, nor did they wait for a large inheritance.
Successful business people are simply the people who went out and did
something ... and then stuck with it.

Some people who read this book will not own a business. They will dream about owning a business, but they will always find a reason or excuse to prevent it from happening. There are others who will take this book, learn what they need to know and then create the future they want. Which one are you? Only you can answer that question. Good luck and remember that everything is achievable if you believe enough in your dream.

Biographies

RICK BISIO

Rick Bisio has earned his reputation as the franchising world's leading teacher and matchmaker by guiding clients through self-discovery, determining *if* – not when – they are suited for business ownership. Bisio's uncanny ability to identify each person's unique interests, skills and abilities has resulted in hundreds of great business decisions across a wide range of industries.

With wisdom and insight gained from his own business-building and from the experiences of his "raving fans," Rick Bisio now shares the secrets of preparing for, identifying, researching and operating successful franchised businesses.

With both Vice President and Director level experience, Bisio was instrumental in growing the Popeye's, Church's, Seattle's Best Coffee and Cinnabon brands into over 30 countries in the 1990's. Since the 1990's, Bisio has been deeply involved in entrepreneurship and investing. He has owned, bought and sold franchises under his own name and with partners, and has assisted others to achieve their vision.

With a passion for mentoring, Bisio committed to sharing his franchising and entrepreneurial knowledge as a coach and mentor though this book.

Bisio earned his undergraduate business degree from Washington University in St. Louis, the Simon School of Business. He earned his Masters in Business Administration/Masters in International Management from the Thunderbird School of Global Management in Arizona. Bisio has also held positions as a teacher and as a public speaker.

MIKE KOHLER

After more than 20 years as a business communication executive with Cox Communications, Mike Kohler was introduced to franchising through his work with Rick Bisio. Kohler has successfully owned both franchise and master franchise businesses. His experiences in franchise exploration contribute an end-user dimension to this book's concepts.

Kohler has taught business management and English composition. He earned his Bachelor's degree in Communications (Journalism) and a Master's degree in Business Administration, both from the University of Nebraska-Omaha.